To Zary,
May you reach your
stars & dreams.
much love & light

Dr. Keith Tong
Jun 19/2022

Cutting Loose

An Inspiring Journey to Becoming a Beacon of Purpose and Love

Keith Tong

Most diligent help with flow, structure, organization and content
by Patricia Colomy

Contents

Preface

I co-authored the book, *Entrepreneur Success Stories*, with my mentor and four-time best-selling author, Colin Sprake, where I briefly explained how I became an entrepreneur. My story is featured in Chapter 2 of the book with the heading, "In Life, What Goes Down Must Come Up!"

After having six near-death experiences I began to question why I'm still living today. So, I went on a quest to find my purpose and why I'm here on this planet. Many readers of *Entrepreneur Success Stories* approached me and told me I needed to write the full version of my life story. They believed the kind of story I've lived could help many people that are dealing with obstacles, downfalls and hardships.

The deep dive into my own personal story and re-living some of the most haunting moments of my life was extremely difficult. Some moments, as I typed out my story, I would break out in sweats. Other times, tears would suddenly roll down my cheeks as I re-lived those traumatizing and horrific events. Recalling those moments was extremely nerve-racking. But the journey allowed me to heal myself by reflecting on my hardships and allowing myself to become vulnerable.

At first, I didn't want to share my story and have people know I was a bum, a crack-head, wannabe gang member and a junkie. I was ashamed. I felt down and dirty. I was weak. I had failed life miserably.

There were many times along the way that I wanted to end my life. There was nothing and nobody to turn to. I lost the will to live many times because I didn't believe or feel I had any purpose or reason to remain on this planet.

When I came to a point in my life where I thought I would never return, I sought deep into my soul; looking for some hope to return back to humanity. I desperately wanted to be myself and to love myself. It didn't happen immediately, but I did manage to find the light I was yearning for so much.

The light was HOPE. The light where my life is much more precious than giving up on myself. This is the light that gave me enough strength to climb out of that dark, cold hole I'd been in too long. It took every ounce of energy for me to say to myself, "I am worthy of living. I love myself too much to end my life. No, you devils, you are not going to take my life away. I am here to stay." I then managed to compartmentalized all the failures and negatives in my life, shelve them and throw away the key.

Things were finally looking up. But just when I thought everything was nice and rosy for me, it all came crashing down in a matter of weeks. I hit the ultimate low in my life. I lost my business, my home and 1.5 Million dollars. I began to ask, "Why is this happening to me?"

Then the past came creeping back slowly. Those fears of failure came creeping up again. The beliefs that I am not worthy of having money, that money comes with great difficulty or that I am not good enough to be successful, all re-appeared again. My past life that I'd kept hidden away began to resurface and I thought to myself, *hadn't these issues been resolved once I threw away those keys?* I soon realized that life doesn't work that way, and since then, my life has been going up and up, after having failed for nearly twenty-two years.

The project of writing my life's story took a little over two years from start to finish; with many edits, refining and some re-writes. At one point, I shelved the project, believing it had served its purpose by helping to heal me of what was remaining and hidden deep inside my soul.

The many breaks I took during this project allowed me to reflect deeply into who I am, why I am on this planet and what I am meant to do. It's important for me to emphasize for my readers that the guilt, the shame and the failures I endured over the years have shaped me into who I am and who I am becoming.

My hope for the reader is that you read with an open heart and open mind. My wish for you is that you feel motivated and inspired to take action into your next evolution in life.

This book is not about getting you rich or providing you with solutions or a roadmap to get rich instantly. It's not a book of all-hype or the same old story you've read in other motivational or inspirational books; those books that get you off your ass, only to have you back on the couch in no time.

I'm just an ordinary guy who fought, punched and sometimes surrendered when life got the better of him. I've made many mistakes along the way, but one thing is for certain; I never gave up.

Like most other people, I'm not in that 5% of the population who are super rich or super successful. I'm part of the 95% of the rest of the world battling it out to make ends meet. And through all of the struggles, I finally realized that *I* create my destiny, my happiness and my desire to live my life to its fullest.

I want to share my story with the public because we are living in a world with so much turmoil and hopelessness. There are so many people ending their precious lives too early. This needs to change. There is hope, and as humanity we are united to help each other. We *must* practice this in order to see future generations prosper and succeed in life.

Later in this book, I will provide you with 10 priceless nuggets that I believe and trust. These nuggets have been taught to me, and I am using them to help attain my highest level in life; aligning my mind, body and soul into oneness. I am certain these nuggets will be tools to help you overcome what's holding you back personally and professionally.

Acknowledgment

My journey towards personal development started with reading books by authors like Anthony Robbins. I soon wanted more knowledge than I could obtain from reading books, so I began attending workshops and seminars. My first real face-to-face experience was with T. Harv Eker. Many years later, I had the privilege to learn from Colin Sprake, Founder & CEO of Make Your Mark Training and Consulting, and Adam and Randi Markel of New Peaks, formerly known as Peak Potentials.

The experiences and tools I acquired from these mentors and coaches provided me with the strength and courage to break through my darkest secrets and fears by looking beyond my limiting beliefs. In doing so, I am now able to teach and inspire others to look beyond and find their own light of hope.

Another mentor that really tested my inner being and watched me grow, allowing me to heal on a deep level physically, emotionally and spiritually, is Marcia Wieder, founder of Dream University, where she defined the word "dream" as a verb. She is a best-selling author many times over, and I was enrolled in her mystery school program, The Meaning Institute, for two years. Being in her program proved to be the most rewarding and fulfilling process. It helped me become who I really am and to fulfill my life's passion and vow. Marcia guided me to open my heart so that I could love the world and more importantly, myself. She believed in me and pushed me to be the person I am today. I am so grateful to have met her and to call her my friend.

Other influential mentors and coaches I must mentioned are Satyen and Suzanna Raja of Accelerated Evolution Academy. Certainly, their teachings and wisdom were a major turning point that accelerated my evolution and desire to make this world a better place for all conscious beings. Currently, I am enrolled in their Mastermind program to accelerate my evolution at a quantum level. Their program has given me the tools and skills that I am utilizing to help my own clients clear their pathways of negative and limiting beliefs, allowing them to get to the next level in their life; a life of true happiness and grace.

Most importantly, I must thank my one and only, my beloved wife and best friend, Helen Tong. We have grown so much together as a couple. There have been many happy moments, but there were times when darkness threatened to sever our strong bond. The universe threw us so many curve balls to test us as a couple, to test my commitment to her and to test my love. She has been by my side through all of my ups and downs. Throughout all the trials of life, she has remained calm and rational. If she hadn't been by my side, I don't know where I'd be now. She has given me the strength and the sanity to move beyond the challenges and look for that light at the end of the tunnel. She is my rock.

Finally, I would like to thank my daughter, Amanda, and my son, Jacob, who have walked alongside my journey and provided me with the inspiration and hope to see this project to fruition.

Foreword

I was introduced to Keith by a colleague years ago and it was instantly clear to me that he was a man of perseverance. He and his wife originally committed to a one-year program with me, which turned into two because of Keith's immense appetite for new knowledge. This was about the time he and his wife were experiencing a great struggle to hold on to their pharmaceutical business, and he was determined to do all in his power to overcome their hardships.

During those two years, Keith took a particular interest in the fundamentals of the wounded child and the power of healing old pains. He knew that this would be his personal key to unlocking his prosperity.

Keith has tackled the road to becoming a doctor with the same voraciousness he showed in my program years ago. He has learned to accept his setbacks and move through them with courage, forgiveness and compassion. His ability to embrace life's chaos and uncertainty has pushed him to levels of success in beating heavy drug addiction, recovering from bankruptcy and creating several lucrative business ventures.

There is no limit to his dedication to improving himself spiritually, physically and financially, and he has chosen to share his story so that others may flourish in the same betterment. This book is just one more example of Keith's great tenacity to live life in his full potential, and I am deeply proud of him for his many accomplishments.

-Marcia Wieder, Best-selling author and CEO, Dream University

Endorsements

"Keith is an amazing person who completely embodies resiliency and tenacity. In times when most would give up, Keith is still at it. He's proven that you can get through anything that comes your way. His advice and experience are something everyone should listen to, as he can lead you through what you may consider to be impossible situations. His incredible journey makes you realize that your trials are merely small bumps in the road to owning your greatness. Learn and prosper from his brilliance."
- Colin Sprake, Founder & CEO, Make Your Mark Training and Consulting Inc.

"Entrepreneurs, read this compelling book to liberate your highest potential! Keith Tong has had a remarkable life journey that has taken him from the depths of despair to the heights of freedom. As you walk in his shoes, through so many twists and turns, you will see a path of clarity emerge to guide your own steps with flow and fulfilment. He shows how you can go from being far off course to coming to your true purpose and power. And you'll avoid many pitfalls on your road to greater success in life and business."
- Satyen Raja, Founder WarriorSage Trainings

"Keith Tong is a Warrior of the Light, a fate only possible by triumphing through darkness. His passion for humanity plus his masterful healing skills are ignited by his global consciousness and tenderly tempered by his humility. Keith is Canada's Deepak Chopra."
- Allana Pratt, Intimacy Expert

"A heart-felt, wise, honest, and tender book. We don't always get to choose what happens in this life, but we can choose to grow in compassion and wisdom as a result. Cutting Loose makes accessible to the reader author Keith Tong's vulnerability. It's encouraging to read a book from such a solid and successful businessman talking about painful life experiences to instead become heaven on earth situations."
- Debbi Dachinger, Syndicated podcast host, international bestselling author, visibility media strategist

Proceeds

All proceeds from the sales of this book will be donated to help the people in the Downtown Eastside, as this was the place I lived when I really thought my life would end. The Downtown Eastside is a place located in Vancouver, British Columbia where droves of people suffer from addiction and mental health illnesses. This was my home when I had nowhere else to turn. It's hard to find the words to describe the kind of place this is, but I will do my best.

The Downtown Eastside is a place where many are homeless and vulnerable. At the time I lived there, it was the most dangerous place in Canada because of the high crime rate related to murder, assault and overdoses. The streets were littered with garbage and the smell of urine was everywhere. It was enough to make an average person nauseous. Everywhere you turned, there were drug dealers and people shooting drugs into their arms as if it were normal.

I feel a calling to help these people because I was once one of them. I, too, suffered from addiction for many years. I resorted to using heroin as my drug of choice, so that I could escape the pain and misery that had tormented me for much of my childhood, teenage and young adult life. These people need my help, just as I had many deep wounds and scars that needed to be healed.

My Life Line

Below is a quick synopsis of my life. As you can see there were many lows within my life. These lows are what I needed to get out of the many holes I had dug myself into. I didn't choose to give up on life, nor myself. I chose to want what's best in my life and my future.

Lows

Lack of money, so living with old clothes dorky haircut; being bullied in school many times over

Dad brutally abused me. Chased me all the way outside for taking a slice of cheese, because I was hungry

Called stupid and dumb by everyone

Repeated 3rd grade (junior school), and got expelled that year for breaking a window

7th grade, my dad nearly killed me for stealing money in school

Ran away from home after getting expelled in 10th grade for hitting a guy

Came back home after some time and had to repeat 10th grade again

Never went to UBC because I had no money

The worst time of my life; I started hanging out with the wrong group of people, got involved with hardcore drugs, became a drug addict, eventually becoming homeless. In jail many times, and lost all hope in the world

Claimed Bankruptcy; 7 years on my credit history

Going to court to battle the government after being in business for about 5 years

Highs

Received 1st place with Royal Conservatory of Music; I am not stupid after all

Started doing well in school once I hit 8th grade (high school)

Got accepted to the IB Program in 10th grade

Met my first high school sweetheart and first love

Moved out with Hans; finished 12th grade (high school)

Got Accepted to UBC

After many countless tries, was able to fight my addiction habit; climbing out of a very deep hole; getting back into society

Got my first job; on the path toward recovery

Met the most beautiful women I ever laid eyes on, who is now my wife, my best friend, and my business partner

Becoming self-employed; a life of being an entrepreneur

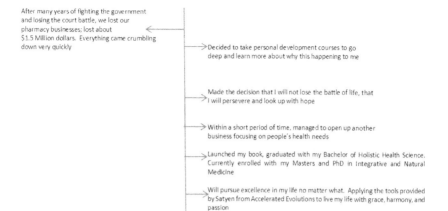

After many years of fighting the government and losing the court battle, we lost our pharmacy businesses; lost about $1.5 Million dollars. Everything came crumbling down very quickly

Decided to take personal development courses to go deep and learn more about why this happening to me

Made the decision that I will not lose the battle of life, that I will persevere and look up with hope

Within a short period of time, managed to open up another business focusing on people's health needs

Launched my book, graduated with my Bachelor of Holistic Health Science. Currently enrolled with my Masters and PhD in Integrative and Natural Medicine

Will pursue excellence in my life no matter what. Applying the tools provided by Satyen from Accelerated Evolutions to live my life with grace, harmony, and passion

Chapter 1: Development in Poverty, Prejudice and Abuse

Living as a Scared Child

My first cries, as I gasped for air leaving my mother's womb, marked the day I began to shape my life. I was born in St. Paul's hospital in Vancouver, British Columbia during a hot July evening. This is where the journey began for Keith Tong.

As a toddler, I was aware of having moved many times from one house to another. My grandparents babysat us a lot because my mom and dad had to go to work most of the time. As I was growing up, there were many more negative events and emotions compared to the few positive ones I can remember.

One of the best memories I *do* have from my childhood is going to Disneyland with my family. I got to see all of my favorite Disney characters, like Mickey Mouse, Donald Duck and Pluto the dog. We were at Disneyland from the morning all the way to the night; going on most of the rides and seeing many wonderful attractions. I remember being so happy and lively as I went around seeing all the delightful characters and all the other kids having fun with their families. One of my favorite rides was It's a Small World. I loved being on the little boat and looking at all the wonderful dolls on display while listening to the cheerful music playing. I remember it very clearly because the ride made me so happy, and that night I fell asleep with the song playing in my head.

Another happy memory is taking a long road trip to visit my relatives in Salt Lake City, Utah. We went to Salt Lake City because my mom wanted to visit her sister who she had not seen in a long time. My dad wanted to get to Utah as quickly as possible, so he only took short driving breaks and laid a mattress in the back of our van for my sister and I to sleep on while he drove through the night. I also remember that in those days candy was so cheap that you could buy a really wide selection for just a few pennies. They came in all shapes and sizes with different flavors. My favorite ones were the Popeye Candy Sticks that came in a small box. I would love to open the package in a particular way, pull one of the sticks out of the box, put it inside my mouth and pretend I was smoking. I loved the way Popeye Candy Sticks tasted in my mouth.

These are the only good memories I have from my childhood years.

Because I come from an Asian background, life with my family meant very few displays of affection or love. Instead, there was lots of screaming and yelling in the house. It came from my dad, mom, sisters and even myself, as I would yell back at them - especially my sisters. If it wasn't my dad or mom yelling at me for doing something stupid or wrong, my sisters and I would yell at each other because we didn't see eye to eye. It was either arguing about the TV channel or someone took someone else's toys, etc. Sometimes, this resulted in being hit by my parents - especially my dad.

While growing up, I found learning new things to be very discouraging and difficult because I couldn't figure things out quickly. I clearly remember many instances where it took a long time for me to understand something new. For example, I was never good at math during my elementary days. There were many times my mom made me memorize the multiplication table and I would forget it within minutes. I would get the answer to 4 x 9 right one minute and then get it wrong the next minute because I forgot so quickly.

My parents became frustrated with me for learning new things slowly. Another example is when I was about five years old and I tried going down a flight of stairs. Now, when people go down the stairs, they typically place one foot down and then the opposite foot goes on the next step. What I would do is place one foot on a step and then place the opposite foot on the *same* step before progressing. I would step like this the entire way down the stairs because I was afraid of falling. My dad kept telling me to stop doing it that way and showed me how it *should* be done. For about a half an hour I couldn't do it and my dad became frustrated and angry with me. He called me stupid and refused to take me to school that morning. My parents always put me down by calling me "no good" and "stupid."

In elementary school I went to a speech therapist because I couldn't pronounce certain words properly. The school recommended this because I had trouble articulating certain vowels or consonants correctly. For example, I had trouble enunciating words that began with the letter "t," such as "tomato." Instead, I would pronounce it as "potato." In addition, there were some words that required me to curl my tongue, which was most challenging for me. I remember my speech therapist being very patient while helping with my pronunciations. I tried really hard to pronounce the words properly, but I just couldn't do it. Another reason I failed miserably and couldn't improve was because both of my parents spoke very poor English. So, the only time I could practice was with my therapist.

There were several simple things I loved to do as a kid. For instance, I loved jumping off sofas and furniture like the superheroes I saw in cartoons. I also loved going down the carpet staircase on my bum, like a slide on the playground.

One thing I really loved to do was jump off the sofa and land on my knees on the carpet. Of course, my dad didn't like that because it shook the house whenever I jumped to land on my knees. He kept yelling at me to stop, but I kept doing it. I was just having fun. He would always say to my mom, "He keeps on forgetting to stop jumping like that! I'm getting tired of this." So, one day, he told her to sew round buttons on the inside of my pants, right around my knee area.

The buttons were a mix of materials: wood, metal, plastic. My mother used whatever she could find. The only similarity was that they were all big. They were the kind of buttons you would find on a heavy winter coat: thick and made to last. It was extremely uncomfortable walking around with those buttons sewn on the inside of my pants.

I was just a little boy having fun and there were times I forgot the buttons were even there. Once, I hopped onto the sofa in the living room and began jumping up and down. The next thing I did was land on my knees on the carpet floor. My entire body weight slammed down onto those buttons. The force of the impact shocked me as it split the skin on my young knees. The pain was so sharp and foreign that I screamed out. I laid on the floor for a few moments, crying and cradling both knees in a desperate attempt to comfort them. I knew I had to see how bad the damage really was, so I sucked up my fear and quickly rolled up my pant legs. I had never seen so much blood come out of my body before. The sight of it only made my tears fall harder and the pain more unbearable.

My parents found me by following the sound of my cries. My mom put Band-Aids over my knees which helped to stop the bleeding. My dad, who was only angered by my noise, told me to shut up and said I'd gotten what I deserved because I didn't listen to him. My mother's care made the moment easier, but taking a bath later that night was extremely painful. The warm, soapy water crawled its way into my open wounds and created an entirely new agony for me. The only thing that stung worse were my father's mocking and deprecating remarks.

The scabs from the injury took weeks to heal, as they would constantly break open and have to rebuild to protect my freshly exposed skin. That was when I started hating my dad for the misery and pain he brought me.

I'd really love to tell you that I learned my lesson the first time those buttons crashed into my kneecaps, but that wasn't the case. It took about a half a dozen more instances before the pain finally wasn't worth the fun. And in the end my father won; he had successfully stolen my simple childlike love of jumping off the couch.

Another time I hurt myself as a child was when I stuck a wire inside the wall socket, zapping myself. I didn't know I wasn't supposed to play with the electrical outlet. I was just playing around, and I got electrocuted badly. Both of my hands and arms turned black from the electricity shooting through me. I cried really hard and to make things worse, my mom laughed at me. Thankfully, my dad wasn't at home or I would've gotten a beating.

Later, my parents decided I should attend a Catholic school because they thought I was a naughty boy. This was around the same time we moved to another location near Chinatown. They thought Catholic school would be good for me, but I hated it so much. I had to wear a very uncomfortable uniform every day, and the teachers were so strict. Plus, the classrooms creeped me out. They weren't like the normal rooms in the others schools I had attended. I remember a time when a teacher slapped me on the face in front of the other kids for misbehaving in the classroom. I just wanted to find a hole to hide in when the other kids teased me for that. It was miserable and traumatizing.

I have two younger sisters, which means I was the only boy in the house. They say in the Asian culture that boys are very important, but it never seemed like it to me. There were many times I wondered why I had parents that always put me down or called me names, like stupid or useless. I would often close my eyes and wish for another set of parents who would treat me with kindness and give me the love I really needed. But when I would open my eyes, things would be the same; no change. Slowly, I began distancing myself from my parents, hating them more and more - especially my dad.

Another thing that really affected me negatively was the fact that money was always very scarce for my parents. Many times, I would ask them for things I wished to have, such as toys or candies and they would say, no. They would always say there wasn't enough money. These very interactions spawned my own limiting beliefs about money.

My Father's, Mother's and Grandparents' Role, Growing Up

My Father

From what I was told by my mother, my father left Kowloon, Hong Kong to seek a better life in Vancouver. I don't know too much about his past or my grandparents. I only met his father once and his mother twice, in my lifetime. When my father arrived in Vancouver, he met my mom and married her at a young age.

My dad also had a brother who I only met twice in my lifetime. He was a highly successful trader in the stock market, from what my dad told me. Many times, I felt my dad was jealous of his brother's success by the way he would talk about him. My dad could've stayed in Hong Kong and tried to make money. Instead, he came to Vancouver to find a life for himself and to settle down.

As I was growing up, I would hear the occasional facts about my dad's early years. One day my dad told me that he was abandoned in the forest at a very young age because his parents thought he was mute, and they didn't want a child that was "defective." So, they left him in the woods to die. I don't know the specific details, but he did end up finding his way back home to my grandparents' house. I sensed much resentment from my dad when he told me that story.

When my grandfather passed away, I remember my dad shedding a few tears and not saying very much. He kept his emotions bottled inside of him whenever it came to things that were affectionate. Of course, he had no trouble bursting with anger or yelling at me whenever something didn't go his way.

One time, one of my younger sisters was acting up and my dad lost it. He grabbed a knife and motioned with it to tell her to be quiet. He lost control of the knife and dropped it. He used his hand to block the knife from falling down and hurting her and ended up cutting himself badly. There was a lot of blood on the floor, and he eventually had to drive himself to the hospital. The cut was very deep and he required stitches. That was an extremely scary moment for me to witness.

My dad was a custodian throughout his entire life. He held a second job where he worked the graveyard shift for a large phone company. During those times, my mom was a stay-at-home mom, making sure dinner was prepared and that we were being taken care of.

As we got a little bit older, there were many times my dad would take the family to help out with work. This was mainly done during the weekends. It became a weekly routine for the family, and it was extremely boring for me. My job was to do all the vacuuming. I spent at least 4 - 5 hours vacuuming the various job sites. Because some of the locations were large, we would wake up early in the morning to get to the site and be home late in the evening. We ate our snacks and lunch at the job sites, and we did this for many years.

At the peak of his career, my father had up to four job sites in Vancouver. On top of that, he was cleaning his boss's house located in West Vancouver every two weeks. Because he was so busy and I had to go help him, I didn't have any social or play time with my friends.

Eventually, those longs hours my dad worked took a toll on his health. He was working very long hours without getting adequate rest or eating at regular times. He started feeling bad and decided to go to the doctor. After a few blood tests, the doctor confirmed that my dad had developed type II diabetes. A very common symptom of diabetes is a very short temper. I think this is one of the reasons why he would take his anger out on me a lot of the time.

Never once when I was growing up was there any quality time between father and son. No love, affection or support. It was yelling and hitting most of the time, which is the main reason I was never close to him.

My Mother

My mom came to Vancouver from China at a very young age. I do not know how she met my dad. I'm much more attached to my mom than my dad. I would always go to her for anything I needed or to be consoled when I was upset. My mother has one older sister, a younger brother and a stepsister. Whenever there were family gatherings for any special occasions, we would either end up at my mom's parents' home or my aunt's home to have a festive dinner. I had some cousins, but I was never really close to them. I usually kept to myself whenever we would meet up.

When my mom found out my dad had developed diabetes, she wanted to get a job. She thought if she worked it would reduce the workload for him. But my dad was adamant that she was not to get a job, since we were still children. He wanted her to stay at home to cook for and take care of me and my two younger sisters.

Whenever there were any severe arguments between my dad and mom, my dad would threaten to divorce her. My mom would always give in whenever he threatened divorce, as she was fearful of it. Back in those days, when one got a divorce it meant being a failure, on both sides of the family. As I got older, I began feeling sorry for her because she felt helpless and fearful of my dad leaving her. There were many times my dad would beat me up and my mom would plead with him to stop. He would threaten to divorce her just so he could keep on beating me. He knew she would always give in to him.

Still, I love my mom and I cannot blame her for not being there for me. She didn't want to risk her marriage failing with my dad. There were many times my mom would tell me not to report my dad to the police or he would end up going to jail. She knew that what my dad was doing to me was wrong, but she didn't know what else to do or who she could turn to.

My Grandparents and Extended Family

I was never close to my grandparents on my father's side. The visits from them were minimal because they were living in Hong Kong at the time. We were always close to my mom's side of the family, since they lived in Vancouver.

My mom's dad was a man of many talents. I remember my mom telling me that he formed an association called the Lee Association in Chinatown to promote the family. He was a goldsmith, a Chinese culinary chef and a tai chi master.

We would often visit my aunt who I called Dai Yee, meaning "bigger aunt," as she was older than my mom. We would visit her side of the family at least once a month. We would have big family dinners at either my aunt's house or my grandparents' house, especially during Chinese New Year, birthdays and other special occasions.

The dinner parties would consist of a variety of homemade food, such as chow mein, chicken, rice, soup and other delicious delicacies. I remember Dai Yee always wore a white apron, which would be stained with hard work and food by the end of the day; the marks of a successful gathering.

Between my sisters, cousins and myself, there were usually many kids there. On special occasions, Dai Yee would give us red envelopes with money inside. I was always excited for this, as it was rare that I ever had my own money. I remember the pride I felt holding those five or ten dollars in my hand. My imagination would spin over the possible goodies that money could bring me.

There were always two or three tables set up for mahjong and I can still hear the clattering of the tiles being swirled around and flipped over onto the tables. The sound of clinking dishes echoed from the kitchen as my mother and Dai Yee cooked. They moved around each other like a dance; keeping time with the rhythm of chopping knives.

Most of the men spent their time watching hockey on the television while the women cooked. Except for my father, who usually found a quiet corner with the Chinese newspaper. From time to time, he would get up and mingle with the women, but he mostly kept to himself.

As a kid, I had to join my parents at these get-togethers, and oftentimes I'd rather have been at home playing with my toys or watching television. But looking back, I do miss the spirit of these gatherings. Most of my family has moved away since my childhood days, and some have passed away, including Dai Yee, who died of lung cancer three years ago.

Many times, when I was very young, my parents would have my grandparents babysit me and my sisters. We were too young to go to work with my dad, at the time. The only things I remember doing at my grandparents' home were watching TV and goofing off. I was extremely bored at their home because there was never really anything to do.

My grandpa was a smoker, and I remember playing around with his pipe. The smell of the pipe was kind of fruity. On sunny days, I could see the cloud of smoke just suspend itself in the air. There were times when I would wave my hand around, making the smoke dance on air.

When I got a little older, I took an interest in martial arts. Back then, my favorite martial arts idol was Bruce Lee. I watched his entire movie collection. My number one favorite movie was *Enter the Dragon*, where Bruce Lee played a spy trying to infiltrate a known enemy.

My dad didn't want me to learn martial arts because he thought I would use it against my sisters. He gave me an ultimatum, insisting that if I really wanted to learn I needed to learn from my grandpa and learn his technique. Well, my grandpa's technique was tai chi, which is a slow-moving form of martial arts. I tried learning tai chi from my grandfather but I soon got bored of it because I didn't have any patience.

I remember getting frustrated with my grandfather asking him why it was so slow. I asked him, "Who fights like that? All the martial arts shows I watch on TV are never this slow."

Then he told me to punch him anywhere on his body. I couldn't believe he was asking me to do this. But I did as he told and in the blink of an eye, I was on the floor. I did that three more times and I was on the floor every one of those times. I was amazed at his agility, since he was such an old age.

My mom had a younger brother who was living with my grandparents at the time. Sometimes I would hang out with him when he was home. He was a tradesman, which meant he was very good with his hands and innovative when it came to fabrication. He had many tools all over the house and in his garage. He even built a little workshop in the garage with many different projects always on the go.

There were times I would practice tai chi with my grandfather in the backyard, while my uncle would be working away in the garage on his projects. Once, my uncle was building a single passenger plane from scratch and I was asking him so many questions. Building a funny car from scratch is another one of his many projects I can recall.

As I got a little bit older, I had to begin helping my parents with the cleaning business and my times with my grandparents were greatly reduced.

My Money Belief System: Elementary School Days

In elementary school, I was bullied a lot. I mean a LOT! No matter which school I went to, the bullying followed me. People at school would pick on me all the time because of the way I was dressed and the way my hair was cut. There was a great deal of racist name calling in my direction on a daily basis in school, as well. There were many times the other kids would call me dorky, stupid or chink.

To make matters worse, I was very slow academically because I couldn't understand what the teacher was teaching. The most difficult subjects for me were math and English. Many times, when I got my report card it was full of D's and E's. Whenever my dad would see my report card, he would yell at me and tell me how much of a failure I was and that I didn't deserve anything good in my life.

Most importantly, I was very lonely in school. The other kids didn't want to have any association with me because of my looks or how I was doing, academically. I was labelled as being the most stupid kid on the block. I barely had any friends, and I yearned to fit in with the rest of the kids.

One day during recess, two boys from my classroom asked me to go with them for a walk. I was so happy and eager that they would ask me to go with them. I remember thinking, *I'm being accepted by some cool dudes!*

I didn't think anything of it when we went off the school grounds. We ended up walking just a few blocks away from school and the two boys asked me to throw a rock into the front window of a house.

"It's cool," said John.

"It's fun," said Peter. "Nothing will happen. Don't worry!"

I trusted them and did what they told me. I broke the window to the house, and by the time the rock hit the glass, the two boys had already run back to school. I heard the glass break loudly and I ran back in time for the school bell to ring for my next class. My heart was racing and pumping so fast. The two boys just laughed and snickered as I walked into the class room.

Later in the day, I got called into the principal's office with the two boys. I didn't know how the school had found out, but inside the office was the principal and an older lady. The principal informed me that this lady was the owner of the house I'd broken the window to. She came looking for us at the school and pointed me out as the one who threw the rock and smashed her window. From there, the principal called my parents in for a meeting. I told the principal that the two boys had told me to throw the rock.

I was very worried about what would happen to me while I waited for my parents. When my dad and mom showed up, I knew I was dead. I was a goner. I had butterflies in my stomach and my legs were shaking very badly. I was afraid of what my dad would do to me. I could tell, as the principal told them the news, that I would get a massive beating for my actions.

Later that day, I had to go to the lady's home to apologize, and my dad gave her a check to pay for the damage I had caused. I was suspended from school for a week, and when we got home my dad gave me a severe beating; one I would never forget.

My dad then used this event for the next few months to verbally abuse me. He thought I was incredibly gullible and had no will against the influence of others. He believed I would do anything anyone told me to do, without even considering the consequences. And he never missed an opportunity to tell me this. He would constantly say to me, "If someone told you to eat shit, you would do it."

The two other kids who'd encouraged me to smash the window got a light slap, compared to me. One of the boys got suspended for a couple of days while the other one got an ear-full from the principal with no suspension. I got the worst of the punishment, since I was the one who threw the rock and broke the glass. When I came back to school after my suspension, the kids in my class didn't want to talk to me at all. Even worse, the two boys that got into trouble with me began bullying me.

One of the boys had some karate training and one day he used one of his moves on me. I was running toward him in anger, because he had been calling me names, and he moved to one side and hooked his leg causing me to land flat on my face on the gravel field. Eventually, I began crying because I wasn't able to get back at them.

That year was the worst year for me because of all the shit that happened; the bullying and the constant abuse from my parents. Meanwhile, my schoolwork suffered because of all this. I failed third grade and had to repeat it the following year, meaning I was now one year behind in school. My parents were extremely disappointed with me and would further torment me because of it. I was not allowed to go out to play with my neighborhood friends at all that summer.

Because I had to repeat third grade, my parents thought it would be better if I changed schools, so they enrolled me in another school that was further away. They thought this would give me an opportunity to start fresh and maybe try to form *any* friendship. I told them I hated the previous school because of all the bullying and teasing I had faced.

Although things at the new school were somewhat better, things at home became worse. There were so many arguments at home that it became unbearable. I learned to tune out all of the yelling, and I found ways to block all the verbal abuse coming from my parents. In our culture, spanking was considered okay as a form of discipline, so physical abuse was the norm in our household. However, my parents went far beyond the norm.

A strict rule at home was to ask for permission before going into the fridge. One day, I was very hungry and I forgot about the rule. I went directly to the fridge, found a piece of sliced cheese and ate it. When my dad saw that there was a slice of cheese missing, he got pissed like I'd never seen before.

"Who took it?" He demanded to know.

From the tone of his voice I knew I would be getting another beating, and I reluctantly admitted my guilt.

"I did," I said.

He then started to hit me hard and shake me violently. I started crying out loud. I remember him grabbing something really hard and hitting my arm with it. He kept on hitting me and hitting me until I ran outside screaming. I was hoping somebody would help me. My neighbor, who was an older gentleman, heard me and came out.

"What is going on?" He asked.

I was crying and hurting from so much pain that I couldn't answer.

My dad followed me outside and told the neighbor it was none of his business and he should go back to his home. The neighbor told my dad to stop hitting me. My dad's response was that he had a *right* to hit me and that he can do whatever he wanted. The neighbor told him to calm down and that I was just a kid.

In the end, the neighbor was unable to do anything to help and he left. My dad then grabbed me by the ears and pulled me back home for some more beating. I was in so much pain and hurting deeply inside. I contemplated killing myself many times because I didn't want to face the pain and brutal beatings any longer.

By the time I was around 11, I wanted to do something different that would change my situation from all the constant yelling and beating. I really wanted to do something that would please both of my parents. Because they enjoyed classical music, especially my dad, I decided to learn to play the piano.

My first interaction with the piano was through an after-school activity for anyone who wanted to learn how to play. Because there were days I was walking home from school, I decided to try it out on my own. I really liked it and wanted to take lessons, but of course I needed my parents' permission first. When I asked them if I could take lessons, I knew my dad wouldn't allow me to unless my sisters were involved somehow. I really believe that if my sister had said no when my dad asked if she was interested in learning to play piano with me, he wouldn't have paid for my lessons.

Over time, the after-school lessons became inadequate for all three of us to learn piano. So, my parents managed to find another teacher for us. My parents were pleased with my progress because my teacher always told them how good I was. I enjoyed playing the piano because it allowed me to express my emotions into the music. The teacher harnessed my natural talent at the keyboard and I expressed the flow of the music through my body and fingers. I became good at it. I started to have confidence in myself because I was expressing the music physically.

My piano teacher told my parents that I had a gift for music and was very good. She encouraged my parents to keep pushing me to play. I remember a time when she was teaching me the skill of playing the melody while using my body movement. The way I did it made her laugh, but she went on to say that I was doing it perfectly.

As I was playing the piano, one thing I needed to do was play in recitals and compete with fellow pianists. I was in third grade at the Royal Conservatory of Music and I was competing with about fifty other piano players at the time. I had to sit there for over three hours waiting for my turn and listening to the others play their pieces. It was a very tough, very long wait and rather boring.

When it was my turn, I got up on stage and looked at all the eyes looking back at me, with the judge in front. I started to get nervous. But once I sat down on the piano chair and proceeded to have the music flow out of me gracefully, I forgot about all the people. I just played and played. When my piece ended, I got up and bowed. People were clapping, as it was a courteous gesture to do so.

There were ten more people that needed to perform to complete the recital. It took about an hour before the results were released by the judge, as he needed to take some time to write things down and go over his findings. There were only three prizes: third place, second place and first place. It was tradition that the judge started by announcing the third-place winner, then second and finally first.

At the time, I really thought that I wouldn't win anything at all. I thought I was an okay piano player; nothing special or worthy of winning first place. Both my mom and dad were there because they really enjoyed listening to people playing the piano. As the judge started with his speech, he expressed his gratitude and appreciation for all the performers and said there were only going be to three people to claim prizes. As he started with the names, I noticed myself sinking further and further down in my chair.

The time came when the first prize winner was to be announced. The judge spoke loudly, "The first-place winner is Keith Tong of third grade Royal Conservatory."

When he spoke my name, I looked around to see if there was another Keith Tong. Then I remembered from the itinerary that I was the only one with that name. I looked at my parents, then over at my piano teacher who was also there at the recital. I couldn't believe it. I got up and walked down to the stage to receive my prize from the judge. He congratulated me and went on to tell the audience how much he loved my piece because I played it well and was able to express the melody with my body and fingers.

This was a big turning point for me because it gave me a boost of self-confidence and it proved to me that I was *not* stupid. I showed my prize to my school teacher and fellow class mates. They were all surprised with my achievement.

I had gone from first grade at Royal Conservatory to third grade, completely skipping second grade, and graduated with distinctive honors. I skipped another three grades and made it to the sixth with distinctive honors again. After that, I progressed all the way up to 10th grade. My piano skills, up to 10th grade, took me about five years to attain. That was a big achievement to reach in such a short period of time.

My grades in school started to improve once I started playing the piano. I guess once I knew how good I could be at playing piano, I realized I could be doing well in school, too. By then, I was in ninth grade and I dreamt of becoming someone of importance, like a doctor or a successful business person.

I could've continued on with piano lessons, but the practicing became very long. I would practice for about an hour and a half to two hours daily because the music was very long and I had to practice all the finger exercises. I didn't want to play piano that long everyday as I started ninth grade, which was high school.

As my homework load increased, it took more time for me to finish and I had less practice time with the piano. Since my two sisters were also playing piano, I had to wait in between their lessons and mine. During the evening, the piano would be playing from after school right into bedtime. It became unbearable for me.

Although it was my idea to start piano lessons, I soon hated it. Every single day there was constant nagging and bickering about how long I should be practicing. Because of this, it became more of a chore rather than an enjoyment. It felt like playing piano was only for my parents' pleasure. Not once, in those five years of playing, did I get a day off from my lessons. It became a mundane task to always please them this way. No matter how much I did or how hard I tried, they were never satisfied with my efforts.

Soon after getting to high school, I hated playing the piano because of the practice time. I couldn't go out with my friends because I had practice to do. My dad kept me at home like I was in jail. I was not allowed to go out anywhere except with him and my mom.

I mentioned earlier that my parents had switched piano teachers. Well, that came at a big price. The new teacher was very expensive. In order for my dad to pay for the three of us to continue piano lessons, he ended up taking on a second job. This was another reason my dad and mom always pressured us to play piano; because of the amount of work they had to do in order to pay the teacher.

Throughout my childhood, my parents' money situation was always very tight. Personally, I think their priorities were in the wrong place. There were things my parents wouldn't provide for us that I thought should've been necessities. My dad should've taken on another job to get the things that would have made the whole family happy rather than making himself happy by putting us through piano lessons.

Money was so tight for us that my clothes were always outdated or too short around my ankles. Most times my shoes were so worn out, there were holes in the bottom of the soles. My haircut was awful because my dad would take me to a stupid barber in Chinatown to get it. It looked like he put a bowl on my head and just shaved around it. The kids at school would always laugh at me because of the kinds of clothes I wore or the way my hair was cut.

Because of the lack of money, I could never get the things I wanted for myself. When I was in sixth and seventh grade, the Transformers cartoon was a very big hit on TV. Kids came to school with these toys that could transform into many different shapes and sizes. They were mainly machines that would transform into robots. The good guys in the show were called the Autobots, and their leader was named Optimus Prime. The bad guys in the show were called Decepticons, and their leader was named Megatron. All I knew was I wanted one of those toys. Many times, I asked my parents if I could buy one, but they always said no. I always envied my classmates who brought in toys that I could never have. I wondered why they were able to have the toys that I couldn't. It wasn't fair at all.

Then, one day, I had an opportunity to get some money for myself. I happened to find out that the secretary of the school put their cash inside a filing cabinet. I noticed that the school office door was open and no one was around. Like a sneaking cat, I cautiously walked into the office to see if there was anybody around. I remember saying, "hello," out loud just to make sure. When I determined no one was around, I opened the filing cabinet and the bag of cash was inside the bottom drawer. I took the bag of cash and hid it inside my jacket.

I left the office making sure I was not seen. I went down a passage way that led out of the school and was not regularly used. My heart was racing as I left school grounds. I found a hiding spot in a wooded area behind the school and proceeded to open the bag. I had never seen so much money in my life! I bundled it into my pocket and I threw the bag away where I was hiding. I cannot remember the exact amount I had, but it was a lot. I went home quickly and hid the money away, downstairs in a space where no one would find it.

The next day at school, I was called into the office. The principal and vice-principal were suspicious of me, but I denied it. They stated that somebody remembered seeing me in the hallways at the time the money went missing. They called my parents in to explain the situation, and I continued to deny everything.

My dad kept insisting that I had stolen the money. He thought I had done it because I was always lying to him. I had learned to lie to my parents in order to keep from getting hurt. I felt lying was the only way to protect myself from them.

A few months had passed and I'd spent some of the money on a couple of Transformers toys and a watch. My mom asked where I got all the toys and I said that my friends lent them to me to play with. As for the watch, I told her that I found it outside on the street. She thought I was lying, too.

As the weeks progressed, my dad started to look all over the house for the money, and it drove him crazy that he couldn't find it. It took a few months, but eventually he *did* find it. He and my mom called me downstairs where he had found the money, and the next second, he grabbed me by the shirt and began beating me badly. I thought I was going to die. He grabbed my head and bashed it against the bricks of the chimney furnace, yelling at me, "Die! Die! You are not my son! I want you to die! I don't care if I go to jail, you are going to die! Die, die!"

Because of the way he bashed my head against the chimney, by its corner, my head began to heavily gush blood. My arms and legs were in severe pain and very bloody. I remember him throwing me around like a ragdoll and within minutes, I blacked out. When I woke up, my mom was protecting me so my dad would stop. She pleaded with him to stop so he wouldn't end up killing me.

My parents didn't take me to the hospital because my dad didn't want to face the doctor. He knew they would ask questions which would lead to a police investigation, as there were so many bruises all over my body.

For many days I couldn't wash my hair because my head hurt so much, along with other parts of my body. There was so much blood on my head that it took weeks for it to come out of my hair. This happened during the summer so I had no school. I just stayed home and nursed myself back to health. It took months for me to heal, physically. To this day, you can see the scar on my head where my dad brutally beat me.

Within two months of that traumatizing event, my dad started giving me an allowance. When he asked why I took the money from school, I told him that all the other kids got allowances and they got to have toys to play with. I told them it wasn't fair that all the other kids got an allowance while I didn't.

Despite his decision to grant me an allowance, I hated my dad after that ruthless beating. I felt helpless and didn't have anybody to turn to. I hated life and everyone around me. I didn't want to have anything to do with my parents at all. I knew I had to leave home because I couldn't tolerate this kind of treatment any longer.

Reflection: Growing Up During My Childhood

As you can see my childhood days were very sad and traumatizing. To relive those events and write them out on paper sent shivers down my back. There've been times where I had to stop typing and walk around to let the emotions flow out of me. Other times, as I described an area of my childhood, tears would flow down my cheeks out of nowhere.
 Growing up was horrendous for me. There were many times I wanted to call the police and report my dad for child abuse, but I

was scared. And I was scared for my mom. I didn't know what the future would hold for me if I had done that. I didn't know if I would be separated from my family or where I would go. So, I just stuck it out as long as I could.

Nugget Number 1 for you is this: Many of the debilitating thoughts and beliefs that keep us from success, stem from adverse influences and events in our childhood. In order to convert these negative ideas, we must first recognize where they come from. After that, it's a matter of working on letting forgiveness and compassion into our hearts so that we can address these thoughts and beliefs from a place of love. Only then can the negatives be transformed into positives.

There've been many instances and events that unfolded during my childhood that created many limiting and negative beliefs.

To name a few:

1. I don't deserve money
2. I am not worthy enough
3. I am stupid and dumb
4. I am not good enough
5. Money doesn't come easily and I have to work really hard to have it
6. Nobody loves me

As I reflect back on those moments, it's no wonder I kept on hitting road blocks in my life. For me to change my negative and limiting belief system, I needed to work on several things: I needed to know who I am and acknowledge who I am by opening my heart, and I needed to allow love and compassion into my heart.

Thanks to Marcia Wieder of Dream University and the Meaning Institute, I was able to open my eyes to this. And by doing so, I was able to forgive myself for anything that happened to me, and to forgive others for what they may have done to contribute to the creation of my negative beliefs. From there, this is what it looks like for me now:

1. I deserve all the money, now and onwards, filling me with abundance of many kinds
2. I am worthy
3. I am bright, clever and intuitive
4. I am always good enough
5. Money comes to me easily and freely; I do not have to work hard for money
6. The world loves me and I love my life

Chapter 2: Old Wounds Run Deep

High School Days: Negative Influences by My Peers and Parents

Eighth grade was the start of my high school days. Being new in school was an opportunity to meet new people and friends. I felt this would be a whole new chapter of my life. What was great was the fact that all my elementary school peers were going to another high school that was in their catchment area. Since I was living outside that catchment area, I enrolled in a high school that was only three blocks away from my home.

I was happy for my new opportunity. It was like a switch inside my head turned on, and I suddenly took an interest in my academic studies. I wanted to do good in school by getting A's and I participated in many after school activities, such as debate, chess club and badminton. I had dreams of becoming successful and having lots of money. I didn't know exactly what that would look like, but I felt it inside my body.

During that time, I dreamed of making big money, having the freedom to do whatever I wanted and having all the things I wanted out of life. Setting up a solid foundation for myself in order to do something good in my life became a priority for me.

I took eighth and ninth grade very seriously. I studied hard and I did very well in school. I even made it on the honor roll, and I started to get out of the house more often. Sometimes, I would even stay after school just to hang out with the new friends I had made.

I went to the malls once in a while and to the school dances they held a couple of times a year. I was always trying to convince my parents to let me go out whenever there was an evening event in high school. It felt like I was in jail because they controlled my life;

telling me what to do and to stay home all the time. As usual, I would have screaming matches with my parents or my sisters. Sometimes all of them at the same time.

When I was in ninth grade, a group of friends talked about a program being launched on the West End of Vancouver called the International Baccalaureate Program or IB, which started in 10th grade. It was talked about as one of the best programs to be in, and if you completed it, any university would accept you as first priority. There would even be a scholarship issued upon graduation, depending on the university. This program was only offered at one school in Vancouver at the time, which was about a 35-minute bus ride plus a 5-minute walk away.

There were many requirements that needed to be met in order to be accepted into the program. One of the prerequisites was to be a well-rounded person. They didn't just want bookworms or nerds who only did well academically. You also needed to be well-informed about current events, be sports oriented and make some kind of contribution to society.

One of my friends challenged me to apply for the program, and I accepted the dare. I needed a challenge, and I wanted to prove to my parents and myself that I could do it. At the time, I played badminton and participated in track and field. I was also very advanced in my piano achievements. All of these skills and achievements helped me with my application to IB.

The application also required me to take two standardized tests and sit down for three different interviews with different people. I was so nervous. There were many applicants for the IB program during that time, including two friends of mine from the same high school.

While I was taking the standardized test, I counted at least one hundred applicants in the school gym. It would take a few months for the school to get back to us. My parents weren't too thrilled because if I got in, it meant I had to commute about forty minutes by bus to get there. I would be further away from them, and it meant they had to spend about $50 a month on a bus pass for me.

Months went by and I was really anxious to learn whether or not I'd been accepted into the program. One day, I received a letter in the mail. The letter head was from the school. I was really nervous when I saw it. I held the letter in my hands, closed my eyes and prayed for good news. Careful not to tear what was inside, I slowly opened the envelope.

Inside, the letter read, "Congratulations!" I had been accepted into the IB program at this renowned school! I couldn't believe my eyes. I had to pinch myself, rub my eyes and re-read the letter a few times to make sure it was true. I jumped up and down with joy. It was the best news I'd ever heard. That moment, I told myself that I was not stupid after all. That I was worthy and could achieve anything, if I put my mind to it.

The next day, I told my friends I had been accepted. I even showed the letter to one of the friends who thought I couldn't get in. Only two of us had gotten in. It was a boost of happiness and appreciation to know that I was now part of something worth pursuing. Look out 10th grade, Keith Tong is coming to town!

I couldn't wait for ninth grade to end because I wanted to start the IB program *now*. I was already tired of my current school. I had a few more months to go and the days seemed to drag on longer. Some of my close friends started to become jealous of me and I didn't know why. I asked them why they would treat me like this and told them they should be happy for me. I worked so hard to be where I was and to be in that position. Soon afterwards, I stopped talking to some of them who treated me poorly. I didn't need those kinds of people in my life.

Starting the IB program filled me with excitement, yet I was not sure what I was walking into. I had some moments where I thought I wouldn't last because of the uncertainty that came along with it. I began asking myself if I was up to it and would I be able to pass the exams as the term went on.

When I started at my new school, I noticed right away how many more Asians, I mean Chinese people, attended. I had been living in East Vancouver all my life and Asians were not the norm. We were a small minority group in my old school compared to this one. Thankfully, I was able to converse a bit in Cantonese, as the students all around were speaking the language during class, in the hallways and outside of school. The people in this new school were supportive and friendly, and it made me want to fit in.

Soon after, I took an interest in people that were labeled as "cool" around the school. What I mean by cool is the way they dressed, how their hair was styled, etc. For example, some had slicked their hair to one side or wore it spikey looking and some of them smoked cigarettes. They distinguished themselves from other people by calling themselves F.O.B, or "fresh off the boat" kids. I was so drawn to them because of the way they looked and acted. I thought that was cool.

I soon took on that "coolness" myself from the group I started to hang out with. First, I started skipping school, which was a big leap for me. I never skipped class in my old school. Second, I found the level of academic difficulty to be substantially higher than my previous school and I started thinking it was too hard. Rather than trying harder to understand what was difficult for me in some of my courses, I chose to have fun with my friends and to feel like I fit in.

After adopting my newfound coolness, it didn't take long for me to start smoking. My first breaths of that cigarette made me sick to my head, yet I took a few more drags. I remember having quite a buzz in my head and things becoming sort of dizzying for me. Smoking became a habit in no time, as I felt it was cool and I really wanted to fit in with my new buddies.

I also became very interested in cars, especially the ones that were decked out and souped up with body kits and sound systems. Imported cars started to take off because one could do so much with them. They looked great and they were super cool.

Because I hung out with the cool dudes, my status and role in the school became very important. It felt awesome to belong to a group of like-minded people who shared activities and desires. I just wanted to be part of a group where I counted for something.

As the IB program progressed, my grades suffered. I skipped classes too often, didn't hand in my assignments on time or didn't do any homework at all. I was falling behind very quickly. Trying to be cool with my friends took precedence over my grades. Another big distraction was the number of pretty girls at this school. The ratio of girls to boys was something like three to one.

All the exuberance I had felt when I first started the IB program had begun to fizzle. The notion of keeping up with the cool crowd and belonging to an influential group quickly became my priority. Fast cars and pretty girls filled my focus, and I had forgotten all about my longing for academic achievement. It's remarkable how fast our desires can be swayed with the right motivation. Or the wrong influence.

Running Away from Home at Age 15

One cloudy day, right after school let out, a group of us were hanging outside in front of the school, checking out the girls and admiring some of the cars. One of my friends saw a guy he didn't like and usually picked on for something he did or for the way he looked. My friend approached this guy and started to push him around the school grounds. The guy kept trying to walk away, but my friend kept going after him, pushing him around harder and harder.

Things soon escalated. The guy wouldn't retaliate or say anything in response, so my friend told me to hit him. I don't know why he asked me to do that. I didn't want to do it. But he kept on insisting that I punch the guy because I was part of this crowd. He continued to pressure me, calling me a coward and a chicken for hesitating.

I knew I had to hit this guy or he would start to think I was some sort of chicken, too. So, I approached him. We both had about the same build; a bit smaller than average and athletically thin. I had never hit anyone before, but the excited cheering from my peers took away my nervousness. I just squeezed my right hand into a tight fist and swung. There was a slight *pop* as my hand connected with his left cheek. His face was rather skinny and hard, and I felt his bone collide with my knuckles. I could hear my heart pounding in my chest with adrenaline as he quickly dropped to the ground.

My friends shouted in approval, and I felt a swell of pride rush over me. The guy got up and began to cry as he ran toward his home. We just stayed put and laughed at his retreat. This was the first time I had ever been on the *giving* end of bullying. I wasn't the one being laughed at or being called a chicken or useless anymore. It was finally *me* who had the upper hand and the opportunity to fit in with the cool crowd, which I wanted so badly.

The next day the principal called my friend and I in to find out what happened. Apparently, the guy I hit had not shown up for school. He feared for his life and thought it would happen again. His parents called the school to complain to the principal about the incident, and the school launched an investigation. There was a zero-tolerance policy with this kind of stuff and I didn't know about that. This was my first time involved in an incident regarding school fights. After the principal spoke with us, there were a few witnesses that reported the incident. My friend got a five-day suspension, and I was kicked out of school.

I was completely devastated. I did not know what my parents would think of me. They would've said, "we told you so," looked down on me and told me how stupid I was for throwing that punch. I didn't know what to do next. I didn't want to go back to my old school because I feared I was going to be humiliated and disgraced. I didn't want to face my parents and get into a fighting match with them, either. So, I ran away from home, fearful of what my dad would do to me.

When I ran away, I was sleeping at different people's houses here and there. Some of the places I hung out at were in various local malls, Chinatown, a variety of pool halls and another area called the Projects that was near Chinatown. The people I stayed with were either friends from school or friends of a friend I had met somewhere along the way.

This is when I started all my bad habits, like acting cocky, smoking cigarettes and smoking pot. I met many people along this path, and I even got into trouble with new groups of people. I needed to make some money to support myself, so I teamed up with some people that would help me. I was either selling firecrackers or doing some side deal jobs. There were also people who felt sorry for me and would lend me money whenever I asked.

One time, while I was hanging at a pool hall in Chinatown, two police officers approached me. My parents had filed a missing person's report because I hadn't been home for some time. I couldn't remember how long I'd been away from home because I lost all track of time and was having fun. The police hauled me back home to face my parents. When I got there, I didn't want to talk to them. My mom was so happy to see me when she opened the door. My dad, on the other hand, just took one glance at me and walked away. Within a few hours of being home, cleaning myself up and changing my clothes, I packed myself a bag of things I needed and left home again. I left for a few months, living at different friends' houses for the time.

In the late 80's and early 90's, Asian gangs started to become a presence in Vancouver. There was the Lotus Gang, the Red Eagles (a branch of the 14K's in Hong Kong), the Viet Chings, the Mo Chays and The Gum Gong Brothers. Eventually, other gangs from other backgrounds appeared, such as the East Van Saints and Los Diablos. There were so many gangs on the streets of Vancouver that fights between them were unavoidable. The Lotus members and the Red Eagles were constantly fighting with each other.

I got into trouble with some of the Red Eagles members because they didn't like the way I looked. There was an incident with one member who didn't like the way I was looking at him. I didn't mean to give him an offensive look. My eyesight wasn't that great, which meant I had to squint slightly in order for me to see. Of course, that didn't matter to this guy who thought I was looking at him the wrong way. So, there was a conflict with him right from the start. Oftentimes I would meet him and his gang of friends in the mall and we would have a confrontation. Other times when I saw them and I was by myself, I had to run away quickly to avoid getting beat up.

It became a regular occurrence to look over my shoulder to see who or what was behind me to prevent me from getting jumped.

Some moments were quite scary because they would come out of nowhere and attack. There were a few instances where some of my friends were attacked, as well. However, this didn't prevent me from socializing and having fun.

I had my first experience with pot when I was 15. I remember many times I was partying, making new friends and smoking lots of pot. I even tried LSD once, but I didn't like the effects. It lasted about 48 hours and I didn't like the trip.

Eventually, I got tired of sleeping on my friends' couches. It was a lot of work to pack what I had and then beg my other friends to let me sleep at their home. I couldn't do it any longer. Some nights, when I didn't have any place to go, I slept on the streets. Some nights it got very cold. Other times, I wouldn't be able to shower for days.

About four months after running away, I felt lonely and longed to be home again. I was 16 now and I missed my mom's home cooked meals, my bed, the hot showers and clean clothes. I didn't know if my parents had given up on me, but one day, I decided to call home and ask if I could come back. My mom answered the phone when I called. She was very happy to hear from me and when she heard I wanted to come back, she told me to come home right away.

I didn't know what to expect when my dad opened the door. He just looked at me and walked away. My mom was there to greet me, though. She welcomed me back and told me to go shower. She laid out some clean clothes for me to change into. It felt really good to take a hot shower and be clean again. When my dad went to work later that day, I had a chance to talk to my mom. She had been worried sick about me and said she had spent many sleepless nights worried about whether I was safe or hurt.

She told me that a few days before I called to come home, she had found a dead robin in our back yard. She took the time to bury the bird and as she did, she prayed to the bird that I would find my way back home when I was ready. I felt really bad for having put my mom in this kind of position. Not knowing what to say to her, I just started to cry. She asked me why I ran away from home. Was it because of something they had done or something they couldn't provide for me? I told her that I couldn't stand my dad and that I needed to get away. I was sick and tired of all the yelling and the physical and emotional abuse he put me through. I told her that I'd had enough. She went on to say that my dad would change and that I just needed to give him time. After our short conversation, I assured her that I would not be running away from home again.

Reflection:

As I pondered the reasons as to why and what led me on this path, curiosity of the mind came up. I needed to explore and wonder what life would hold for me. I had dreams and hopes that someday I would become successful.

High school is a very important time because it's where we start to realize what our interests in life are, what life direction we will take and what career path we want to walk on.

Of course, our peers clearly have strong influences over our lives. Do their opinions matter? Are you strong-willed enough to say no? Or to say yes? The kind of peers I had growing up led me on a path of destruction and self-defeat. They helped further re-enforce the limiting beliefs I had about myself growing up.

Some of these included:

1. I am not smart enough
2. I am not good enough to go to that school
3. I cannot do it
4. I don't have the support of my friends
5. Life is just too hard

Clearly, these beliefs I had about myself needed to change and it took many years of healing, personal development training and support from my loved ones, like my soul mate, Helen, to help me change all that.

I want you, the reader, to know that you need to say no to what is limiting in your beliefs or to people that are not serving you in a positive way. I know how painful this may sound, especially if some of those people are ones that you hold close to your heart. I needed to distance myself from my dad because I couldn't have him shape my future his way. That could never happen. I'd rather live a life of true purpose and passion than to try to please others, only to be rejected and tossed aside, like some childhood toy they had outgrown.

Nugget Number 2 I present to you is this: When life throws something that catches us off guard and knocks us down, most of us call this a failure. With that in mind, most of us would stay down, not choosing to get right back up and move on.

Oftentimes, we give up on our dreams and goals all too easily because that's the easiest choice we have. We don't know what the future holds so we end up staying in our comfort zone. But those failures in life shape us into what we will become in our future. Adversity, and dealing with adversity in a positive way, will pave a path to success and happiness.

So, the next time you get knocked down, say thank you to the universe and get back up. And when you get up, get up taller and stronger because next time it will be much harder for life to strike you down.

Hans; I Was an Easy Target for Him to Prey On

The following September, I went back to school after spending nearly a year off. Because I had dropped out of 10th grade, the school district of Vancouver required I repeat it. This meant I was now two years behind in school. I didn't like it, but I knew I needed to get my high school diploma and move on to a university degree. I still longed to become a successful person, to be known to the world and to make a positive impact in society.

I enrolled in another school outside my catchment area because I didn't want to see my old school friends and be embarrassed by them. It took about 45 minutes to get there by bus and metro. I found it really difficult to get used to being in school again. I had trouble concentrating and completing my homework on time. Sometimes I slept in and was late for school. But this time, I wasn't going to fail.

While I was going to school, I took a job as a kitchen prep and cook for a fast food restaurant in downtown Vancouver. I would work Thursday nights and weekends to earn some extra cash to buy some things for myself and have some spending money. I didn't want to ask my parents for money all the time.

Traveling back and forth between home, school and work soon became a routine and I met the same people coming and going. Halfway through 10th grade, I met a much older gentleman who was very nice to me. We met while waiting for the bus home from the Skytrain station. I would frequently run into him after finishing my shiftwork at the restaurant, and he was always polite whenever we bumped into each other. He would offer pleasantries, like, "hi" and "nice to meet you." I would reply back with a polite response like, "nice to meet you, too."

It only took a few months to become fond of Hans. I found him very interesting and easy to get along with. As I grew to like him, I also grew to admire him for his wisdom, knowledge and life experience. He was sort of a father figure; the missing father I really needed in my life. At the time, I was becoming more distant with my parents, especially my dad. I barely talked to him or even said hello. Despite my mom's prediction, my dad had not changed. The arguing still continued and I was arguing more with my sisters, too. It was like the entire family was ganging up on me; like they all hated me.

Soon afterwards, I began hanging out with Hans, who had become a new friend. I found out his place was just two blocks away from my home. His background was European, he was divorced and had no kids. He was about to retire from his work as a jeweler, and he rented an office in downtown Vancouver because most of his clients were nearby. Occasionally, I would visit to see what he was doing and what his job involved. Before I knew it, I was hanging out at his place just to kill some time and get away from home.

He was an avid photographer, and as a hobby he took photographs of things randomly, like people, nature and beautiful architectural buildings. It was wonderful to watch how he enjoyed taking pictures of people and nature. He explained to me that taking these kinds of pictures gave him peace and brought some kind of meaning to his life.

There were many things that drew me close to Hans. He was nice to me; he would listen and offer advice and guidance. He never yelled or screamed at me. Instead, he would bring up a meaningful dialog with me all the time. I started opening up to him and mentioned what had happened; how I had missed school, but still yearned to go to a university. He inquired about my relationship with my parents, but I didn't want to get into it. I think he knew.

As my friendship with Hans grew stronger, he made me visualize and feel my dreams. Because of him, I started to really take an interest in school again. Occasionally, we would visit the university where he developed his films and was a member of a photography club. I was so impressed with all the different faculties. It strengthened my resolve to become a doctor because I had a particular interest in biology.

One night I got into a bad argument with my mom and dad. Upset, I took off from my house and went to Hans. When I arrived, he asked what had happened and why I was so upset. I told him and then I just sat there. It was quiet for at least five minutes. Then, I asked if there was anything he could give me to help calm me down. He said he had something and got up looking around his cabinet for it. He gave me a pill and said it would help me relax. I took it from him without questioning anything and before long I was out like a light. I don't know how long I was out for.

When I tried to wake up, I was very drowsy and I was completely naked. All my clothes were off and Hans was lying beside me on his bed. He was caressing my penis and I told him to stop.

"What are you doing?" I groaned.

"I am making you feel better. Do you not like it?"

"No," I said. "Can you please stop?"

"Why?" He asked.

"Please stop. I don't like this feeling. I still want to sleep, Hans. Stop."

He insisted, telling me that it would feel good. I continued to tell him no and that I didn't like it at all. I tried to resist but I physically couldn't, and I fell back to sleep again. It must have been the pill he gave me. When I came to, I didn't really know what had happened, and I didn't question anything. It was like my memory of the event was totally erased. I didn't remember a single thing.

Sometime afterwards, things had become unbearable at home, and I couldn't take it any longer. Hans knew I was suffering, so he sat me down and suggested the possibility of becoming my guardian and getting a place together. I wholeheartedly agreed. But before that could happen, Hans needed to get permission from my parents. So, he met with them to discuss the idea.

He told my dad it was the best option since my parents' place was small and there was constant friction on the home front. It would be best for me if I moved out of the house with Hans as my caretaker while I completed my final two years of high school. Both of my parents agreed since they liked Hans very much.

Since he was already getting social assistance as part of his retirement, Hans had to go on welfare in order for me to live with him. This way the government could subsidize a one-bedroom place for him. He suggested I take the bedroom while he slept in the living room.

Hans assured my parents that he would be a good influence on me and that I would complete high school under his watch. He and I enjoyed many things together, like watching ass-kicking movies and we were both Trekkies. I spent nearly my last two years of high school living with Hans.

As time went on, we eventually parted ways and I ended up moving back to my parents' home. A few years later, he had some trouble with the law in Vancouver and was charged with sexually assaulting a minor.

Around that same time frame, I got called into the police station regarding Hans. They told me that he was involved in a sexual case with a minor. They knew I had stayed with him at some point in time, and they wanted to know if he had ever sexually assaulted me. I told them no, although I had an odd feeling in my gut that something did happen to me one night.

Hans was charged with various counts of sexual assault, but he was acquitted because there was not enough evidence to proceed with the charges. One day, he phoned me and told me that he was moving to Toronto because he was sick and tired of Vancouver and all the attention he was getting from the police. My parents and I took him to the airport to bid him farewell. I was sad to see him go, as he was the only person that meant so much in my life at the time. Once he left, I lost all communication with him.

Reflection:

I feel it's very important to share with you, the reader, that I had no memory of the assault until I started writing this book. As I stated in the Preface, there were many times I became emotionally overwhelmed while writing out the events of my life. Uncovering this buried memory was the most difficult moment in reliving my past.

A few years ago, around Christmas time, my family and I took a trip to Whistler. I was laid up with a broken foot, so while the family was out running errands, I would stay behind in the hotel room and work on my story.

One day, I was typing away on my computer, describing the moment where I left my parents' house in anger and ran to Hans. I wrote out the part about asking him for something to help calm me down, and suddenly I began to sweat and my mouth went dry. I knew instantly that my body was trying to tell me something, but I wasn't sure what.

It took me about two solid weeks to finish writing this small portion of the story. Every time I sat down to continue, my core temperature would rise and my armpits would be drenched in sweat. My body was sounding some sort of alarm and I knew I had to keep writing in order to understand why.

The memory started to come back slowly; fragments over time. I tried to dismiss them at first, assuring myself that my dearest friend could never have done something like this to me. But eventually the images and sensations were too strong to deny. I felt betrayed and humiliated. At first, I started drinking heavily to try and hide the memory away again, but it was impossible to cover up. This horrible thing happened to me, and my body *needed* me to confront the matter and deal with it.

I truly believe that whatever pill Hans gave me before the assault had helped to bury this experience. I also believe that I kept myself in denial because it felt impossible that Hans could have hurt me like this. For a large portion of my life he was the only person I could turn to. When I felt I had no one to listen to me or care for me, Hans was always there. I loved and trusted him like a father.

Being able to share this moment of my past was a very important part of my healing. At the time the memory resurfaced, I was a part of Dream University, owned and facilitated by Marcia Wieder, which played an imperative role in my healing. With their help, I was able to open myself up with love and compassion and speak the truth.

The suppression of something this traumatic is not to be taken lightly. I want my readers to understand that even though we may not consciously remember our traumas, our bodies will.

Suppression causes negative emotions to course through our bodies, and the stress can eventually turn into sickness and chronic diseases, such as cancer, diabetes and heart failure. We must all learn to confront our traumas from a place of love, so that it can no longer do us harm. This was something that took me years to learn, and I couldn't have done it without the help of my mentors, coaches and loved ones. My hope is that after everything life has taught me, I will be able to help people let go of their pain, just as others have helped me to release mine.

Another Near-Death Experience: The Car Incident

During the last years of high school, I skipped in between classes quite often. The high school I attended had a local coffee shop about a block away that many of my fellow classmates would frequent. A few doors down from the cafe, there was an Italian restaurant that had a few arcade games. If I wasn't in class those were the two places I would go and hang out.

One cloudy day, when it was almost time for school to end, I was with a group of friends having a cigarette outside school grounds. At the time, most of my friends were starting to get their license to drive and one of them drove up in a big white van. We asked him how he got the van and he told us that it was a company vehicle for his job as a delivery driver.

A couple of my friends thought it would be cool to hop on the hood of the van and have him drive down the street. I was a little reluctant at first, but I asked the driver to go slow and he assured me he would. So, I proceeded to jump on with them. I took my position on the hood, nearest the driver's side with my feet resting on the bumper and my hands gripping the roof's edge. My friends lined up similarly along the hood toward the passenger side.

At first, the driver was moving slowly, as promised. But suddenly, he gunned it! I felt the engine growl and heat up under me, and the wind began whipping around my ears. The van was gaining speed, going faster and faster along the street. A surge of nervousness jolted through me. My fingers were squeezing the roof so tightly they began to sweat, and I was starting to lose my grip.

I yelled as loud as I could for the driver to stop, but he couldn't hear me. I had to analyze my options. I knew that if I let go and jumped out in front of the van, he would run me over and I would be dead in an instant. He was going so fast there wouldn't be enough time for him to stop. The only logical thing for me to do was jump to the side and hope for the best.

If I don't let go now, I'm gonna die. The thought was so loud in my head. I held on as long as I possibly could, but eventually I had no other choice. So, I jumped as I finally lost my grip. I flew through the air for a few seconds and then heard the thud of my body hit the ground. I bounced several times; tossed back and forth, like a rag doll between the earth and sky. I had kept my eyes open to try and judge my landing, but everything happened so fast that all I saw were the colors of the clouds and grass rotating as I rolled; gray… green… gray… green. It felt like an eternity.

I hit the concrete a few times before my momentum finally slowed and I came to a stop, laying on my stomach. I stayed there for a moment, afraid to move. I heard the drumming of my friends' sneakers running toward me and I knew I must be alive.

I started to get up slowly, moving one limb at a time, making sure I was in one piece. My friends helped to lift me up and as I stood, I noticed my pants were stained with grass from the impact. I was a mess and in so much pain. There was blood along my body and I was sure I'd broken a bone or two *somewhere*. But after checking myself, I discovered I only had some bad scrapes and bruises. I was unbelievably fortunate.

After catching my breath, I looked around and saw the van coming toward us. The tires had left hot rubber tracks behind them on the street, and I suddenly remembered that I'd heard them screech to a stop as I'd flown through the air. The driver pulled up and asked if I was okay. The second he got the answer he'd hoped for, he sped off.

It took almost two months for me to fully heal from all the bumps and scrapes of the incident. This was one of the scariest moments of my life. For a few seconds, I truly believed I was going to die. This stupid decision nearly cost me my life.

Chapter 3: One Step Away from Gone

My First Love

The first love of my life was a grade higher than me in high school. We dated for about three and a half years. We had many ups and many downs. One thing in particular that put a lot of stress on our relationship was the fact that she hated my dad. One time, he caught us sleeping together in my bed and he began calling her every bad name he could think of. We tried to explain that we had only hugged and kissed, but he didn't care. In his eyes, we were wrong. So, he continued to insult and disrespect her until she cried. From that day forward she hated my dad and refused to go to my home.

My girlfriend was a person that brought light, love and meaning to my life. She didn't have to take that kind of abuse from my dad. My mom really adored her, and I loved her dearly, but because of my dad and the fact that she would be finishing school soon, our relationship started to turn sour and we began arguing a lot.

As time progressed, she went off to college and we were apart at different schools. It became difficult to see each other and this put an entirely new strain on our relationship. We both needed to make some income, so oftentimes we would miss out on seeing each other over the weekends because we had jobs. I started to get scared. I didn't want to lose the person I loved most in the world. I wanted to hold on to her as tightly as possible. I expected her to come visit me all the time, and I didn't understand how important her education was to her. She said I was selfish for placing these types of demands on her and for not supporting her future and feelings.

I felt that we were growing apart and soon she started to become a different person. She began saying things like my maturity level wasn't in line with her expectations and pointing out moments where I disrespected her. She started telling me that I behaved like a kid all the time and that I never thought long enough before acting.

Eventually, she broke up with me. I really didn't even see it coming. I understood that things were becoming tenser, but I didn't think it was coming to an end. I was completely devastated and lost all motivation and drive to succeed. It took so much out of me, emotionally, that I found it difficult to focus on my courses. But I wanted to prove to her that I could still graduate and that I wouldn't be a loser.

I was so angry with her for breaking up with me. It didn't seem fair at all. I found out later that my roommate, Hans, had called her to try and talk her out of breaking up with me. Because it was my final year in high school, he said to her that I needed to finish strong. He was fearful that the breakup might cause me to drop out of school again. But that didn't happen because I was so adamant on completing high school.

There was a graduation prom that followed the ceremony, and it was customary to have a date, but I didn't have anyone to go with. I had asked a few girls but they already had their dates picked. I was disappointed because I had nobody to go with. Everyone else went out and partied after the graduation ceremony. I wasn't in the mood to celebrate, so I went home right afterwards to hide in my room and cry on Hans's shoulder. He felt really sorry for me, as I was still feeling the effects of the breakup. I felt lost and all alone.

Sometime later, my ex-girlfriend called me and said that she wanted to get back together. She said that she had met a guy who was much older than her, but that she didn't really like him and that I had more heart. We talked a little bit about marriage and what it would look like. But during our conversation, my dad came into the picture again, and she said she could never forgive him. We never got back together.

It took me years to get over her, and it was a very hard time for me. It seemed that every time I had something good in my life, whether it was money, friendship or love, it was only a matter of time before I lost it. Things always felt one step away from gone, and I began to see the chaos surrounding me.

Reflection:

Reliving this portion of my past was also a moment of great insight for me. This breakup was a very painful part of my life, and years after, when I first started sorting it all out, I understood that most of my negative behavior in the relationship stemmed from fear.

Coming from a family that showed no affection, it was difficult for me to find strong bonds and love, so I was jealous of anything that took her attention away from me. I didn't want to lose her, and I was selfish because I wanted to be with her all the time. I hadn't really received much nurturing as a child, so it made sense that I had demanded it strongly from her.

It wasn't until I started writing this book and retelling the story that I could see there was more to my behavior than just my insecurities. I remembered that throughout the rockiest parts of our relationship, she often told me that I was just like my dad. At the time I didn't agree with her or know exactly what she meant. But looking back, I can see that the effects of my father's abuse had reached me on a much deeper level than I realized.

I had witnessed him mistreat and manipulate my mother for so long during my childhood, that I treated my loved one in the same selfish manner. I had always pushed my needs to the front of our relationship and had no concern for the pain I could be placing on her, just as my dad had done to my mom.

The wounds of abuse can run deeper than we think, just as any other trauma. It can be buried so deep in our subconscious that we think it plays no role in our suffering. But these hidden pains can have a great impact on our thoughts and actions. Our pain should not be shrugged off, but confronted, so that it can be understood and finally freed from our body.

A Dream That Didn't Come True

In the final months of 12th grade, a classmate in my biology class approached me, asking if I ever wanted to own my own business, be my own boss and make a lot of money. She went on to say that there was a business opportunity she wanted to introduce me to.

"Hey Keith," she said, "I have an opportunity I want to discuss with you where you could be your own boss. You want to check it out?"

"Sure," I replied. "What's it all about?"

"It would be too much for me to explain, but we're having an event where this person will tell you all about the opportunity. You open to hearing more about it?"

At the time, I didn't have anything more to lose, and I've always been open to learning more. I was hoping this opportunity would be something that would prove to my ex-girlfriend that I was capable of becoming successful.

"Okay, when is it?" I asked.

"Let me check the date and I'll get back to you."

"Okay, I'll check it out. I got nothing going on right now."

Later, she drove me to the meeting place. It was in a high school and there were hundreds of people gathered in the auditorium all dressed up in suits and ties. We ended up sitting in front of the stage.

At the start of the meeting, a gentleman walked onto the stage and started talking about himself achieving his dreams and goals. Then the auditorium lights dimmed and a video began playing. It was a video that portrayed a luxurious lifestyle that included fancy cars, large mansions and beautiful locations with all sorts of beaches and sunny places. I had to admit, it was one of the best videos I'd seen that really motivated me to pursue my dreams and aspirations. This was a video of endless possibilities; only if one worked towards them.

When the video ended, another speaker came on stage. I was glued to his message. Everything he said resonated within me. The opportunity he introduced was a network marketing company called Amway. He taught the concept of building a team in order to leverage other people's effort and time. So, rather than having 24 hours in a day, you would have 36 or 72 or even hundreds of hours in a day. This can only be achieved when you start enrolling people underneath you, which is called downlines. In turn you are really duplicating your efforts because, like you, the team under you also has dreams and aspirations they want to achieve.

This concept made sense to me. If I found 3 people to join my team and they each found 3 people, then I would have 12 people in my organization, and I would benefit from all of their efforts by getting credit for their work. This is the power of leveraging. I found this concept to be perfect. I would not be working hard, but working smart. It was a no brainer for me, so I enrolled in the program. There was an upfront charge and a monthly requirement for me to continue onwards with this opportunity.

"It's like owning a business without the headaches," they pitched to me. I wouldn't have the stress of paying for utilities and rent. And since I was now self-employed, some of the expenses I incurred could be written off for tax purposes. I was so motivated! I wanted to change the world and I wanted to be rich.

I attended many meetings and functions with Amway, and I had to travel across the border to the United States for huge quarterly and semi-annual conferences. I met a guy who was from the same city I was and who had recently become a Diamond Director. At just 18 years of age, he was the youngest guy to have ever achieved that. That meant he was earning some outrageous income at the time. I think it was close to seven figures, once he included all the bonuses he earned along the way. He was smart, charismatic and an excellent speaker. He would go up on stage without breaking a sweat. It was second nature to him. I idolized him and wanted to be just like him; even better.

I was very involved with the program for about six months when I started to run out of steam. I was getting frustrated because I was not seeing any results. The concept they sold to me was incredible, but very difficult for me to sell to others. I found it extremely hard to find people who wanted to work with me and to create a team atmosphere. I did manage to find some people for my team, but they quickly ran out of steam, too.

Eventually, I lost interest in this opportunity. I heard from other people that it's just wishful thinking for anybody to reach these kinds of levels in the program and be earning a six-figure salary in such a short period of time. "It's practically impossible," some of them would say to me.

I told myself there must be an easier way to make money. I was very motivated to become a successful person and I needed to find other ways to make money. I didn't give up on the concept of network marketing, however. I just told myself that this company was very difficult to be successful with, as you had to meet lots of people and put in many hours of effort before you saw *any* results.

Mid-way through 12th grade, I had applied to various universities and colleges. There was also a program offered to help students find out what career interests they have. Based on the questionnaire I answered, there were only two areas of interest that stood out for me: being a doctor and being in business. My chart score showed those two interests were very high. Even the counselor made a comment that it was the first time he'd seen that kind of result. It was rare.

I received a letter one day from a local university stating that I had been accepted to their Faculty of Science program. I was really happy with that, but I wasn't looking forward to it. I needed money to afford my tuition and books, and I wasn't about to ask my parents for assistance. So, I threw away my dream of going to a university. I didn't have the money, the motivation or the reason to get my degree.

When I was no longer involved with school and Amway simultaneously, things became different. I had graduated, I was single and I was trying to build my team; I loved meeting new people. I started to go out on a daily basis, partying a lot, smoking pot more than usual, getting drunk and just having fun. I guess I did it to escape the pain I was still feeling from the break-up. Yes, once I graduated high school, it was party time. It was a blast.

This behavior is what eventually forced me to move out of Hans's house. We had started arguing a lot, and we couldn't see eye to eye any longer. So, I moved back to my parents' home and continued my party habits. But losing the love and support of Hans really took a toll on me, emotionally. He was the only person who knew how much pain I'd gone through my whole life, and he really stood by my side and supported me. It was the only relationship I'd had that encouraged me to succeed and made me feel safe.

In my search to fill the void that losing Hans had left in my heart, I met many new people. Unfortunately, most of them turned out to be the wrong people.

Reflection: During My High School Days

With a somewhat shaky and traumatic childhood, I really only had two choices: my parents' way or my way.

The world we live in is based on two polarities, or two dualities: Right vs. Wrong, Love vs. Hate, Dark vs. Light, My Way vs. Your Way, etc. And we, as beings, cannot experience one without knowing what the opposite feeling would be.

Do I live the dreams my parents would've wanted for me or do I pursue what I think would be best for my life? Being a teenager allowed me to find out what I was longing for and the kind of person I wanted to be. Whether it was my girlfriend, my peers or my way of living, I had dreams and aspirations to be the best I could be.

When that all came crashing down, I allowed myself to become the victim rather than the victor. Often, I told myself that I *should've* done it this way or I *could've* done it that way, resulting in many regrets along the way. This kind of thinking expends a lot of energy and took me on a path of negative outcomes and disharmony towards myself, further strengthening my limiting and negative beliefs.

So, Nugget Number 3 is this: We all have dreams and aspirations, but there's one thing that constantly gets in the way: we're living in a world of chaos and uncertainty. Recognize this, we cannot feel chaos and uncertainty without being comfortable where we are now. We need to accept the two polarities: Chaos and Uncertainty vs. Being Comfortable in Our Comfort Zone.

Oftentimes, life throws punches and jabs at us to see if we are awake. Typically, we ignore those signs and just become living zombies, only focused on the surface, nothing deeper. Many people don't like living in the unknown because they don't know what tomorrow holds for them. So, my reader, when chaos and uncertainty start to set in, do you face it or do you succumb to the status quo and take the easy way?

To focus on achieving your dreams and your goals means doing the thing you have never done before. To become successful and have a life of harmony and grace means to embrace chaos with love, compassion and serenity. Only then will chaos begin to make sense and become comfortable. To know, is having the strength and courage to step into the unknown.

Let me ask you this, what is some of the chaos and unknown you've faced in your life? Write each experience below and ask yourself, what decisions did you make? Did you succumb to the status quo and give up on yourself? What were some of the outcomes? Please use an extra sheet of paper, if you run out of space.

Life in the Fast Lane: Into Drugs & Jail

Hitting 19 was a very big thing for me because I was legally an adult, in Canada. I was legally able to go to night clubs, buy cigarettes and hang out with the older crowds in pool halls. I also got my license to drive. My very first car was an older import, which got me around. Life was awesome! I had freedom, and nobody could tell me what to do or when to do it.

However, all these freedoms required one thing: money. Through the resources I'd developed along the way, I was doing some small jobs that involved breaking the law to earn the cash I needed to support my lifestyle. As the money came in more frequently and in larger quantities, I started to become greedier. I needed more money.

I got involved with some people that were peddling drugs, mainly cocaine and heroin. The money was so easy to get. All I had to do was meet up with the customers and exchange the drugs for cash. Eventually, my curiosity set in. I started wondering why so many people were using these drugs, and I started experimenting with them, myself.

I started to smoke a bit of crack here and there, thinking it was nothing serious. When I took my first hit, I became addicted instantly. The thing I dreaded with smoking crack was the end of the high. It was awful. Once, I was jonesing so bad I was actually on my hands and knees looking for something that looked like crack. I ended up finding something that resembled it and when I lit it up, I realized it was a piece of dirt.

On the street, there were slang names for the drugs I was dealing. The street name for cocaine was Number 3, heroin was Number 4, and the combination of both was Number 7 (3 + 4). There were several different ways to take the drugs. To ingest heroin, you place a small amount of powder on aluminum foil. You don't have to use very much, just like a pinch of salt. You place a lighter underneath the foil and then suck in the smoke through some makeshift tube, like smoking a cigarette. This was called chasing the dragon and you could feel it right away. It gave me an instant high and I just wanted to nod off peacefully.

Another way of ingesting heroin was to snort it up your nose, which I did not like. You could also mix the heroin powder with some tobacco, roll it in paper and smoke it like a cigarette. The last way, which I found eventually, was to inject it into your arms resulting in a high that was quicker to attain and longer lasting.

Cocaine was pretty much the same way except you could also cook it into a rock using baking soda. The only two ways to ingest this rock is to melt it, either into a glass pipe or some other apparatus, like a soda can. When you light up the rock, it's the vapor you are inhaling that goes into your brain to give you the instant high.

As for number 7 (a combination of cocaine and heroin), you can only cook it into a rock. The high you get from that is completely different. I also heard you could inject it, but I never tried that.

As I got deeper into the drug trade, I ended up digging myself into a deep hole that could've ended my life many times. My addiction to drugs had gotten out of hand. I was literally smoking all my profits away and making no money. Later, those who I called friends were using me as a mule to traffic and transport drugs to their clients. The associates I was working for gave me free drugs as one of the perks. They wanted me addicted to the drugs so I would have to listen to them and be their scape goat, and so they could make me do things I didn't want to do. I was trapped, scared and lonely. I didn't know what to do. If I ran and took off, the people I was working for would easily find me and perhaps kill me or beat the living daylights out of me. I was already beaten badly once for trying to leave, so I didn't dare try that again.

On one occasion, while I was in jail for a length of time, I had the worst withdrawal symptoms I ever experienced. I got extremely sick from it. It was the most horrendous and painful experience I faced. Imagine having flu-like symptoms but at a ten-times level! The constant stomach cramps, the cold, the back pain, shivers, constipation and vomiting lasted the entire week I was in jail. I remember one of the inmates telling me that I was out cold for almost three days, not eating or drinking anything. I think the nurse may have given me something to help, but I couldn't remember anything.

Another downturn in my life took place with some of my drug trade buddies at the apartment I was renting. I was doing a deal with a friend I'd known since high school. He had also gotten involved with the drug trade, as it was easy money. There was a loud knock on the door, and before I knew it, somebody with a big sledge hammer busted down the door. It was the cops. A swarm of undercover police officers raided my place. I counted at least 12 cops. I was scared shitless because I had a gun hidden inside my mattress, that I was holding for one of my associates, and an ounce of cocaine.

This wasn't the first time I'd been caught by the police. A few months before, I was ambushed by police on the street while I was stopped at a red light. I already had a drug conviction and I didn't need another one.

The police that busted my door were from the serious crime division of the RCMP detachment, and they'd received a tip that I had a weapon inside the apartment. They were very aggressive and threatened that I would go to jail for a very long time if I didn't tell them where it was. Eventually, I caved and showed them where the gun was hidden.

The people in the apartment with me that night all got charged, but I got the worst of it. The biggest offense I received that night was possession of a restricted firearm, which is an indictable offense.

An indictable offense meant serving a minimum of two years in jail if found guilty in a court of law. To make things worse, Driver's Services of BC suspended my license because I had too many traffic violations. They penalized me with about $5,000 in traffic fines and gave me a two-year driving prohibition. *How much worse could this get for me?*

After the arrest, the police charged me with drug trafficking, possession of narcotics and possession of a dangerous weapon. They took me to jail that night. By this time, I was using heroin on a daily basis to help me sustain my lifestyle. So, the withdrawals during my jail stay were even worse than the last time. I don't even remember passing out when I got to jail. I remember waking up on the floor in the janitor's room because the jail was overcrowded. Once I was awake, they put me into another cell with other inmates awaiting trail and court hearings. I was allowed one phone call, and I called my sister to arrange bail because she kept a stash of money for me at the time.

When I got out of jail after the third day, I went straight back into the lifestyle, even though the judge had given me many conditions while I was on bail.

Some of those bail conditions were as follows:

1. I was not to carry a cell phone
2. Not to possess any weapon
3. Not to continue my association with one of my other associates in the drug trade

The next day, I found out that the owner of the apartment I was renting had thrown all of my stuff out into the foyer of the unit. They evicted me and gave me 24 hours to remove all that was left of my belongings. Whatever I could salvage, I brought to my parents' house. The remainder, I just left there since I had no other place to keep it. I lost about $8,000 in belongings.

I was all out of options and had nowhere else to go. I was forced to beg my dad and mom for the mercy to give me one last chance. I told them that I had become addicted to heroin and cocaine. I was a walking train wreck. I was lost and felt hopeless. My dad agreed to take me in, under two conditions. One was that I had to quit smoking and the other was that I was not to go out at all. Since I had nobody else to turn to and no other options, I agreed.

The withdrawal symptoms from the drugs lasted for about four weeks in my parents' home. They knew what I was up against, but they wanted me to completely withdrawal from the drugs. What made it very difficult was the fact that I couldn't have any cigarettes during the process. The combination of both really sent my body into shock. The flu-like symptoms just wouldn't go away. I pleaded with my dad to let me smoke cigarettes, but he said no.

I only lasted about a month before I had to find a way to get out again. I got bored at home in no time, so I left again. History was repeating itself. I was recruited by a new group of guys to use my expertise and knowledge of the drug users in the area. Some of the guys knew where my parents lived and they knew I was hooked on drugs. They used the drugs to convince me to work for them. In no time, I was hooked back into that lifestyle again.

It's a known rule of thumb on the street not to take customers from another group. If I "cut someone's grass," or in other words, took their customers away, other drug-trade members would hunt me down and give me a beating, even kill me. I learned this the hard way. When the associates I used to work for found out that I was cutting their grass, four of them found me in a drug house I was living in and beat the living daylights out of me. I'd already received a beating once before, but this time was worse. Once again, I found myself bloodied and bruised everywhere.

At that point in life, I was naive, gullible and weak. It was so easy for me to get used and abused, and I was starting to realize how dangerous the drug industry was. It was a cut-throat market that could get somebody killed, including me. I was addicted to drugs and couldn't see it as obvious as it was. I was only thinking about my immediate gratification; to get a quick fix so I wouldn't get sick and to escape all the misery and pain I'd endured.

I had numerous criminal charges that took years to deal with. I had to attend various court dates to set up trial dates. What usually happened was my lawyer and the prosecution team would set up times and dates but then there were constant delays. It's a frequent practice in the court system.

The court office I had to go to was within blocks of an area called the Downtown Eastside; an area where drug addicts from all walks of life congregated and lived. This place was a last resort for people desperate to get high. It was a dangerous area noted for its poverty, drug trade, sex trade, crime and homelessness.

I had to walk past this place in order for me to get to my court hearing. My curiosity began to set in, so I wandered around the area. I'd heard the drug trade was rampant and accessible. I thought I could give myself another opportunity to make a few extra bucks by peddling some drugs down there. I reached out to a so-called friend of mine who still had connections in the drug trade. He was my last contact that I could count on. He knew I had various charges and was hesitant to deal with me. I begged him to give me a chance because I owed him some money and promised to pay him back.

While I was peddling heroin in the Downtown Eastside, I met some people living on the streets who introduced me to another way of ingesting heroin: the needle. They told me my high from the needle would be ten times quicker and longer lasting than from smoking it. My curiosity set in again and I went ahead and tried that route to get high; I never smoked to get high again.

I didn't know what I was doing or why, but I wanted to stick that needle in my arm. Whether it was coke or heroin, I would jab that needle in my arm. I spent more and more time in the Downtown Eastside to support my habit. I initially sold drugs down there thinking I could make some money, but I ended up doing it to support my own habit. I soon lost control of my life because heroin was in control my life.

Whenever I woke up, I needed to stick that needle in my arm. Mid-Day I would stick it in again. Then I started sticking even *more* frequently. I started feeling and looking like the people in the Downtown Eastside: worn and broken down. I felt helpless and hopeless, and I had no future. I ended up with track marks all throughout my arms, and I had to wear long-sleeve shirts just to hide them. It looked disgusting.

I didn't know how to get out. I sought some help in a detox center, but that didn't last long and I ended up on the streets, using again. My preference was to remain getting high rather than staying clean. It was like the drugs I was hooked on had an invisible chain. The harder I tried to get off, the tighter the chain would grip me. I ended up in jail a few more times because I got caught dealing, and the charges became longer. This drug life of mine had become a revolving door.

My new home was the Downtown Eastside. I couch surfed in people's homes or in various hotel rooms. Sometimes I slept on a couch or on a floor ridden with cockroaches, bedbugs or flies. Some days, I slept outside because there were no rooms available. I wanted to go back to my parents' place but I couldn't. I felt ashamed and guilty of the situation I had put myself in.

During this time, I had a few overdoses but I came through. However, there was one that really struck me hard. One day, I injected cocaine into my arm and my heart began racing with the adrenaline in my system going into overdrive. I didn't know what the guy had given me, but I knew it wasn't cocaine at all. It was something else. I listened to my body and immediately hailed a cab to take me to the hospital. I went to the emergency area and told the nurses that I may be overdosing. By that time, I was having blurred vision and I was sweating profusely. The doctors quickly took me in, ran some tests and had me under observation for most of the night. After a few hours, the doctors determined I was fine so they released me later that same night. My very next stop was to go find my next fix.

One of my court dates was set for a hearing, and I decided to plead guilty to the various drug trafficking charges and the weapons charge. As part of my sentencing, the judge ordered me to get clean, along with some additional conditions. I was very lucky to have a judge who showed compassion and sympathy for me. She issued a sentencing order for me to go a facility called Miracle Valley Centre, which was a residential rehabilitation center for male drug and alcohol abusers over the age of 19.

The treatment consisted of a three-month, open-ended cycle that included individual and group therapy sessions, addiction education, relapse prevention, spiritual healing and a twelve-step narcotics and alcoholics anonymous program. There were about 170 private rooms surrounded by a beautiful forest. It was very peaceful, and there was no interaction with the rest of the world, as the facility was private.

I met men from all walks of life, battling illnesses that had overrun their lives. Every man had a different story behind his addiction, but we all had one thing in common: everybody had hit rock bottom. We had all lost our families, love ones and possessions. Some of the men in the group had even lost their health. At that time, HIV was becoming a problem among drug users, as many of them would share the same needle. All of the men there wanted to change for something better, and they all wanted another chance at life.

After completing two months in the program, we were allowed to leave for the weekends, so we could slowly reintegrate back into society. We would get to leave on Friday and have to be back by Sunday night. If we didn't show up on time, a warrant would be issued for our arrest.

While I was there, two men left for the weekend and didn't return when they were supposed to. The group started to become concerned for their welfare. I knew these two guys well enough, as I had hung out with them, sharing some intimate stories amongst ourselves. Eventually they did come back, but they had done something they never should have, and their lives were forever changed.

The leaders of the center gathered everybody, and we all sat together in a big circle in the downstairs hall. The two men sat in the middle of the circle, and revealed to everyone that they had partied in the Downtown Eastside and fallen off the wagon. They'd both had sex with a woman, without wearing protection, and shared a needle with her, and they both ended up contracting HIV. It was a devastating experience for everyone. Because they had broken the rule regarding drug use while in session with the Miracle Valley program, they were immediately kicked out. There was no second chance.

While there were more than enough examples of negative behavior at Miracle Valley, there were also many positive transformations that took place, and it was amazing to watch. I would attend Sunday service as part of the requirements to complete the program, and I was introduced to God, or a higher power, through the chapel. My time there gave me an opportunity to look deeply inside myself, to integrate God into my life and to understand why I did some of the things I did.

My god is Buddha, and I didn't tell anyone while I was there. I feared the administration would hold that against me and make my experience very difficult. While reflecting back on my mistakes in life, I had to admit I had a problem with drug addiction. I was in denial that this problem even existed for me. Eventually, I surrendered to God and admitted that I had a problem. That was the most difficult process to face, but something I needed to do in order to start moving on with my life.

Once, while deep into a therapy session, it became apparent to the counselors, and myself, that my childhood played a major role in why I began using drugs. There were countless traumatizing events in my childhood; times that paved the road to my addiction. Drugs were a way for me to escape the pain and suffering I had endured. The anger, the hatred and the misery were all bottled up inside of me. The counselors described me as a boiling tea kettle, waiting to explode at any second. My time at Miracle Valley would be the starting point for me to take back my life, and to be in control again.

Another one of the education processes towards healing from my addiction was to make amends with the people I had hurt the most. The people I reached out to either accepted my apology or didn't give me the time of day. Some of them just hung up on me.

While I was at Miracle Valley, I was allowed to give my family a call once in a while. I called my parents one day saying I was really changing this time and that from that moment on, I was in control of my life. *This is it*, I thought, *I am a changed man now*.

When I hit the two-month mark, I was granted a few weekends to go into the city to slowly reintegrate myself. My parents would actually drive one and a half hours from Vancouver to pick me up and drive me back home. Both of my parents were happy that I was recovering and walking my talk. I looked better because I had gained some weight back, and my recovering complexion made me looked healthier.

Most times, when I was away for the weekends, I went to my parents' house. But one specific weekend, I made a big mistake by calling up an old friend of mine to see how he was doing. I didn't have many friends at the time, so I chose to hang out with him. I ended up falling off the wagon, once again, because I had the urge to use.

When I returned back to Miracle Valley, the guilt was eating me away inside. It was a terrible knot in my stomach and inside my heart. I couldn't keep the secret any longer, so I faced my group and told them what had happened. Because I had broken the rules, I was kicked out of the program. Soon after, I was back in the Downtown Eastside using drugs again. Not long after, I missed another court date and ended up in jail, once again. *This will be the last time I'm ever in a cell*, I told myself. I wanted out of that life once and for all.

Reflection During Those Dark and Haunting Times:

There are no regrets in life, is all I can say. There were many times I failed, trying to get ahold of my addiction. Every aspect of my human essence went downhill when I hit rock bottom.

Richard Branson once said, "Do not be embarrassed by your failures, learn from them and start again." I did not choose to give up on life and just wither away. Instead, I had the courage to get up and try once more. It's not the number of times we fail that counts, it's having the courage to move beyond it, so that it becomes an achievement; it's moving *past* those failures.

Nugget Number 4 for my reader is this: We all have failures in life. For myself, my darkest and most horrific life experiences shaped who I am and who I am becoming. I call these events a gift from God. They allow me to share my experiences, wisdom and knowledge with the world; spreading hope, love and compassion.

Another thing I'd like to add is that whatever failures you are holding on to, you must let them go somehow. What we hold inside of us is negatively affecting us, emotionally and physically. It will become toxic to our bodies. Recognize this, the darkest experience, deepest shame or ultimate guilt we hold on to is what shapes us into who we are becoming. Equally important is the message from these failures that we have to share with the world. This isn't a sign of weakness, rather a sign of strength. It's only when we give up on ourselves that we become weak and let the status quo take us over.

Here are some examples of how you can release negativity from your body:

1. Talk to a friend that you can trust and who supports you
2. Meditate on the matter
3. Seek guidance from a professional
4. You can journal it and then burn it
5. You can reach me to help assist you with this matter

The most important step is to *act* and start this process. Do not just sit on it because it will only worsen for you.

Chapter 4: The Healing Power of Work, Love and Forgiveness

Path to Recovery

While in jail, I found out that my grandfather on my mom's side had passed away, and I wasn't able to go to his funeral. My mom was disappointed to hear I was in jail again and she cried over the phone. I could only say sorry and hang up. I knew my parents had been spending more time with my grandfather as he was getting older. His health was not good, but he had lived to a very old age.

One night, while I was praying and looking up at the ceiling in my jail cell, I had a vision of my grandfather looking down on me. Tears began flowing down my cheeks as I asked him for help. I asked him to give me strength and guidance, and to pave a way for me to get out of the life I was leading. My grandfather spoke to me. He told me to call home and seek help.

Just before I finished my jail sentence, I had asked my youngest sister to be a mediator between my parents and myself. I needed her to help me find a way to go back home. I needed a place to stay once I got out, and I told her I'd had enough of that life and didn't want to go back to living on the streets again. She mentioned to me that she would find additional resources to help me fight the demon I had living inside of me; the life of addiction.

Because my sister pleaded with my parents to give me one final chance, I was able to have a place to stay. I went back home and my youngest sister arranged for me to see a counselor to seek help. I needed to fight my addiction.

The program I was referred to, by the counsellor at the time, was difficult to get into. I had to go through an interview process and then get examined by a few medical doctors that specialized in addiction. This was the Methadone Program, which is a maintenance program to help lessen withdrawal symptoms for people coming off opioid-based drugs, like heroin.

I needed to be on the program for a length of time and I had to see a doctor weekly and pick up my medication on a daily basis. It became habitual for me to go to the doctor so he could check my progress, then go to the pharmacy every day to pick up my dose and get evaluated by the pharmacist to see if the program was working for me.

The daily trip to the pharmacy was like having a ball and chain strapped to my leg. It felt like my life revolved around the methadone program. If I didn't keep up with my medication, the withdrawal symptoms would begin in no time. However, I kept my commitment to the program because I didn't want to go back to my past life of drug addiction, crime and sleeping on the streets. My road to recovery meant not only keeping to regular intervals between my medication, it also meant ending all previous relationships involved with the drug trade.

Towards the end of my first year into the program, the doctor began to slowly decrease my dosage level. I wanted to complete the program, so he began allowing me to carry my doses home. This meant I didn't have to go to the pharmacy on a daily basis, anymore. When the time came for me to quit the program, I decided it was something I wanted and needed to do. Some people have to stay in the methadone program for life, but I wanted no more part of it. I needed to move on with my life.

The success rate for someone fully completing the methadone program was about three out of a hundred. That's only 3%. Well, I did it after being on the program for almost two years. I was one of those few success stories! I had fought and conquered drug addiction with the help of the methadone program and my willpower.

While getting clean and off the methadone program, I also needed to clean up my finances. During my time as a drug addict, I had become reckless with my personal finances. From cell phone charges, to having to pay the remainder of the lease for the apartment I was kicked out of, plus high credit card balances, I ended up owing a lot of money. It was somewhere in the tune of $30,000.

I had no job, nor did I have the ability to pay back the debt to the creditors. They kept sending me letters and calling my parents' house to collect payment. I sought every possible way to pay the debt, but in the end, I had to claim bankruptcy to end the turmoil. Claiming bankruptcy was by far the most difficult decision I had to make. But it was something I needed to do, as I was unable to repay the debt, and I needed a new start. Even though this meant a clean slate for me, it would continue to haunt me, as the bankruptcy would show on my credit report for a minimum of seven years.

The dreams and goals I had before were all lost and gone. My drug addiction took it all away from me. The journey from drug addiction to being fully reintegrated back into society took almost ten years of my life. Occasionally, I would ask myself where I would be if I hadn't wasted those ten years.

Having completed the methadone program would prove to be my biggest achievement in life. I'd done it! I believed I had beaten the drug addiction, as I wasn't interested in going back to that kind of life. I asked myself what's next for me in my new chapter.

At that time, I had many underlying issues that affected me negatively. I had low self-esteem, a lack of self-confidence and I was holding on to major guilt about my past. I felt I had something to hide and I didn't want anybody to know what I had done. After all the abuse I'd inflicted on my body, my physical, mental and spiritual views were at an all-time low. I needed something to pick myself up and get me back on the right path.

I heard from various contacts I would bump into on the streets, or from the news, that a few of my past associates from the drug trade were no longer around. Some of them were killed during gang-related shootings, some died of drug overdoses and some went to prison for life, with no chance of parole. I was very grateful that I was able to get out and walk on the right path again, having the opportunity to start my life all over. I was turning over a new leaf. I had a new outlook on life and something to look forward to.

As I slowly reintegrated back into society, I needed to fit in again and get out into the real world. I still felt at odds with myself, but I attempted to network and meet some positive people. That helped a lot because it reinforced all the positive beliefs that had been missing from my life for so long. I knew I had hit rock bottom, so the only direction for me to move was up.

However, on a few occasions, I would have to watch myself with certain things that could become triggers and cause me to go back to my old ways. I was adamant that I would not go back. It takes the body about two years to completely cure itself of these addictions because it's so deeply embedded, emotionally. The physical stuff may be gone, but the memories of the past get stuck in the mind.

For example, it had been almost two years since I'd been clean, and I was watching a movie with a group of friends one night. There was a scene in the film where a character was shooting up. He heated up a spoon with heroin inside, then he drew the poison into a syringe and slowly pushed the needle into his arm. He then proceeded to slowly inject the heroin into his veins.

Watching this scene was very difficult. It was completely nerve-racking and unsettling for me. Both of my armpits were completely drenched in sweat. There were moments during the movie that I had to close my eyes and squeeze the armrest tightly. I managed to stay until the end of the movie, as I had to find the courage to prove to myself that I could handle it. Later on, I told one of my friends about what happened to me. He was very apologetic, but I told him it wasn't his fault. It made me realized that I still had more work to do on myself, regarding addictions.

I also needed to find a job to earn money as a way for me to slowly reintegrate back into society. I felt very awkward while I was applying to various job postings, as I was scared and didn't know what to do. Nobody would hire me because I had a big gap of time in my work history on my resume. I needed outside help, like a job placement program, to assist me with employment.

As months went by, I called some of my old high school friends just to catch up. I mentioned nothing about my dark past, as I didn't know what they would think of me. At the same time, I was calling around to some previous classmates for any leads on employment opportunities. I needed more in life, and I didn't want to rely on anybody. There were many times I wanted to look for work, but I didn't know how. I had applied for various jobs, but I never got any phone calls for interviews. Most of my friends had jobs, while I was at home. I didn't go to school or work, and if anybody asked what I did, I didn't know how to respond.

One day, I saw an ad in a newspaper for an organization that helps people find work. It was a six-month program, Monday through Friday from 9:00am to 4:00pm. The organization was an employment agency that taught candidates how to answer interview questions, prepare a good-looking resume and to enhance their computer, typing and communication skills.

During my application process, one counselor noted the large time gap in my work history and asked me why. I told him that I had taken a lot of time off, but that I was now ready to look for a job. Luckily, I had some valuable skills, already: I spoke really good English, had a high school diploma and knew how to type. An added bonus about the program was that I was getting paid while learning, which helped supplement my income. It wasn't much, but it was enough for me to get some cigarettes and other consumables.

Many of my fellow classmates were immigrants because the organization specialized in ESL and immigration services. Fortunately, I was pretty fluent in English, so I was granted an opportunity to enroll in the program. I enjoyed making new friends in this group and enjoyed my time with them. Sometimes, we had dinner together and it gave me an opportunity to brush up on my Cantonese, since I hadn't really spoken it for a while. I was finally starting to enjoy my life and become a contributor to society. It was perfect!

Towards the end of the program, I had to do job placement interviews and acquire some work placement hours, as required in order to graduate. I role-played with some of my classmates, pretending to be a job applicant or an interviewer so we could answer any interview questions correctly and with confidence. As soon as I felt I was ready, I went out looking for work. Some of us went to various job banks to find employment, while others searched in the local newspaper. There were also some interesting job postings online. I spent my time dropping off resumes to various potential jobs and faxing to others, as per their request.

One day, I dropped off my resume to a car maintenance and servicing shop. I asked for the manager, who took a few minutes going over my resume and asked me a few questions. Then, he asked if I could start the next day and I said, yes. I thanked him for the opportunity and walked away. As I was walking away, it was hard for me to contain myself. After a few blocks, I was jumping up and down with excitement. It was unexpected, and I was extremely grateful for the opportunity. My friends at the job placement center and my parents were happy for me.

My relationship with my parents was a lot better by then because they realized I was trying my best to straighten my life out. They also recognized the mistakes they had made trying to raise me. Although there were still no signs of physical affection, there was less arguing around the house.

Reflection:

The total time it took to get back on my feet, to say no to the things that no longer served me and to re-learn everything for reintegration was over five years of my life.

This was the time I fought my addiction habits, filed bankruptcy, did some jail time and probation and became what I called "normal." This took a tremendous amount of dedication, effort and willingness to build and strengthen my foundation. This was the beginning of defining who I was and what I would become.

The previous foundation I had from my childhood to young adulthood all came crumbling down. Those four years it took were times of trials, tribulations and errors made, to see if I would fall again.

So, Nugget Number 5 is to see what thoughts and belief systems we have instilled in ourselves. There's a saying: "Our thoughts create our life." If your thoughts are limiting and negative, then you will attract limiting and negative shit in your life.

For many years, if something was very difficult for me to understand or I didn't know how to do it, I thought to myself, *I cannot do it*. I kept thinking small about everything in my life. Then somebody pointed out to me that I should write down an inventory of all my beliefs and thoughts about myself. The ones that were negative and limiting were not serving me in a positive way, so I needed to change my narrative, or script. Therefore, my new thought and belief is: *I can do it regardless of it being hard. I just have to learn, and if I cannot, I will ask someone who knows how to teach me.*

So, for this exercise, take an inventory of your thoughts and beliefs. Then, ask yourself, honestly, if they are holding you back or serving you and write the answer beside them.

Now, circle or highlight the thoughts and beliefs that are limiting and negative. Oftentimes, we just have to reword our narrative and change it from disempowerment to empowerment.

For example, when I was trying to fight my addiction with the constant attempts and failures, I kept saying to myself, *I don't have what it takes to quit my drug addiction*. But I had to be the one to change my story. So instead of saying, *I cannot quit*, my new narrative was, *I have what it takes to quit this nasty habit because my life is valuable and I have much left to do on this planet*.

So, take a moment and start changing your negative thoughts and beliefs into positive ones. Write them down on the lines provided:

My First Real Job Since Returning from the Walking Dead

Because I was the newbie at the auto maintenance shop, I was expected to do the dirty work. My co-workers would put me through the wringer and push me hard, to get the job done. Whether it was cleaning the washroom, sweeping or mopping the floor, transferring grease from one 50-gallon container to another, I did it willingly. I didn't mind getting dirty. I was just happy to have the opportunity.

As a junior lube technician, I was doing all the grunt work. I was also on a three-month probation period, under the labor code of the provincial government. It was a steep learning curve for me because I had never worked with my hands before. I needed to be versatile with tools while working on vehicles, so I kept on trying, hoping I would improve as time progressed.

I faced many challenges along the way. With the things I did not know, I asked my supervisors for more clarification. There were instances my co-workers were impatient with me because I asked the same questions over and over again. I had to learn even the most basic skills from scratch. For example, I needed to learn to align the screwdriver head to a screw I was either trying to tighten or loosen. I found the flat heads to be the most difficult because they have a tendency to slide off the screw very easily. I started learning some terms in mechanics such as, "lefty loosey, righty tighty."

As my knowledge and experience increased, I began to ask less questions. I went so far as to go to the library to learn about the basic components of an engine and how it works. I had to get better if I was to last at this job. I didn't want to fail over my stupidity and a lack of effort. Over time, I realized my greatest strength was interacting with customers and educating them on basic information about their vehicle, in turn extending the engine life of my client's vehicle.

When I first started this job, everything was done manually, calculations were done with a calculator and oil changes were going for $16.95. The cars were very simple to work on, and identifying the different components inside the engine, such as a transmission dipstick or brake fluid reservoir, was easy. Domestic vehicles were the easiest to work on because there's ample space underneath the hood to work around.

I stayed with that company for over five years. I had quickly rose up the ranks and became the store manager during my third year. I was extremely excited because this was something I had dreamed of for a long time. I was dedicated, hard-working and yearned to learn more.

On my days off, or evenings, I ventured into different network marketing companies to meet new people and see if there were additional opportunities to make some side income. The network marketing industry still drew my interest because their concept of duplication and residual income made sense to me. The key was to network and be persistent with the product and service offered.

To further enhance my skills and education, I read lots of books on personal development and sales training during my down time. These included, *Sales Training A-Z*, by Tom Hopkins; *Unleash the Power Within,* by Tony Robbins; *Rich Dad Poor Dad*, by Robert Kiyosaki; and several Zig Ziglar books. I was able to apply the principles of these books to my position as a store manager. One key principle was to always remain positive and focused on the task, no matter what, and to always be open for more. When you can do this, other opportunities will come to you easily and effortlessly.

Many changes occurred while nearing my sixth year in the industry. With newer vehicles coming out, things started to become harder to locate and the engine compartments were becoming smaller, which meant greater chances of skin graft burns because the engine is very hot. However, the biggest challenge occurred when computers started to become mainstream, and the company decided to incorporate a computer system into our work. This was a really big learning curve for myself and most of my fellow staff members.

Some of my co-workers were so opposed to the change that they quit. They couldn't comprehend why the owner wanted to change. For me, it was the opposite. I was fascinated with computers because I knew they were the future. I soon became the guru of our new computer system, as I was positive and open to new adventures and challenges.

The purpose of introducing computers was to help streamline the workload, but more importantly, help manage our clients' vehicle maintenance history. I learned everything there was to know about the new program. The most time-consuming part of it was to input customer data into the system. Most of my employees relied on me to make sure they were doing things properly.

One day, the owner of the company decided to host a Customer Appreciation Day. This was a special event in which we invited a band to play live music, gave free hot dogs, offered special giveaways and slashed prices on oil changes. We hosted, I believe, somewhere in the tune of three hundred customers that day. I was assigned to the computer because I was the only person quick enough to enter all their information and cash them out in a timely fashion. From that day forward, my nickname became Speedy Keith.

While employed with this company, I started a relationship with a woman. I had met her at a party and got to know her over a short period of time. We started going out when she invited me to a Christmas party with some of her friends. I hadn't been in a relationship with anyone since overcoming my drug addiction battles back in the day. I had to rebuild my self-confidence, self-esteem and communication skills, in order to start a relationship.

My last relationship had been the one during my high school days. And what kept me afraid of having a new relationship were the facts about my past, having to claim bankruptcy, having no driver's license, and most importantly, I didn't want to be hurt again. But I really liked this girl, so in spite of my fear, I began a dialogue with her, and soon we began dating.

I was afraid of what she would think of me if I told her about my past. It took courage and strength, but eventually I was able to speak truthfully about the things I'd done. I was shocked to learn that she wasn't bothered by my history. In fact, she wanted to help me out. She encouraged me to find out what it would take to rebuild my credit and get my license back. After some due diligence, I found out that I needed to pay about $5,000 in fines to Driver's Services of BC in order to get my license back.

Even though there was a discharge from my bankruptcy days, it still appeared on my credit report for a period of seven years. That meant that trying to get a line of credit from a bank was almost impossible. Therefore, my girlfriend became a guarantor on my behalf, meaning I could start rebuilding my credit history. In addition, we opened a joint bank account to start saving up for our future. I was also able to take out a small loan from the bank so that I could buy myself a car to drive around. The key to maintaining my credit was to make sure I did not accumulate debt and to always pay my bills on time.

My relationship with her lasted close to three years. We realized that we were not meant for each other, as we had different visions for our future. While having a relationship with her, I'd also met some other people who had ideas and dreams that conflicted with hers. I had become involved with people who had dreams of making big money, which involved growing pot. I wanted to get involved with it because I was also money driven. I still had dreams of making money quickly and I wasn't making enough where I was working. When she found out what I was up to, she didn't like it at all and she broke off the relationship. I think she seized this opportunity because we both knew our relationship wasn't going anywhere.

When we broke up, I was worried about my credit, as she wouldn't continue to be a guarantor. I asked myself, *what will happen with my loans and credit cards*? I called the credit card and car companies to see what status I was in. Because I had enough credit history built up, I was able to carry myself and no longer needed her as my guarantor. I was beginning to see light growing larger, in terms of my finances, and felt that I was now in control.

At that time, there was a company specializing in auto glass repairs and replacements right next to where I worked. I became acquainted with the manager and some of the staff there. Over time, I became bored with being the manager of the oil change company. I'd learned everything there was to learn, and I'd reached the highest income level for that position. I wanted more out of life. I said to myself, *I need a change*.

I needed tougher challenges, a change in purpose and direction and I needed to make more money. I was beginning to think I was hitting a dead end with my current position, so I approached Bill, the manager of the glass company, to see what it would take to work for him and if there was any position opening soon.

"Hey, Bill," I said. "How's it going?

"Not bad," he replied. "How are you?"

"Good. Hey, you have a moment for me?"

"Sure, what's up?" He asked.

"I just wanted to know what it takes to work for you? I'd like an opportunity to work for this organization of yours."

"Okay," he said. "We're always looking for people. Why don't you drop off your resume and I'll see what I can come up with?"

"Great, Bill," I smiled. "I appreciate the opportunity."

I submitted my resume a few days later, and he informed me that if he was to hire me, I would start under the apprentice program and get my journey-man ticket after a few years under my belt. A journey-man ticket is like a certification program I would have to take in order to become a glass technician. I would be able to earn as much as $28 dollars per hour, with benefits. I was really excited about the possibility. In my position at the auto shop, I was making a max of about $18 per hour plus commissions and had no benefits package.

It took quite a long time for Bill to get back to me, so I applied to other places in the meantime. I had other interviews set up, but didn't hear anything back from anyone. Most applications were for management positions in other industries. I considered going back to school again to upgrade my skills, but I didn't entertain the idea of getting a student loan and limiting my income. So, I stuck it out at the car company for another year. I started to hate the place and badly wanted a change. Then one day, Bill asked me if I wanted to work for him.

"Hey, Keith, how's it going?" He asked. "You got some time to talk?"

"Yes, I have some time. What's up?" I asked.

"I've been doing some thinking, and I think it's time I take you on. You still interested in the position? You want to come work for me?"

"Absolutely! I would love that opportunity. When would you like me to start?" I asked.

"Well," he said, "out of respect, you've got to give your boss at least two weeks' notice, right? I know Grant very well, and I wouldn't want to create any friction with him, you know?"

"Of course. I will give him my two weeks' notice. And Bill, I really appreciate the opportunity," I replied.

When I gave my notice, the area manager that had hired me jokingly said, "See you back in three months." Two weeks later, I had my farewell party with the boys at the oil change company, and the very next day I bid them farewell and moved right next door to my next adventure.

Reflection:

Eight years had gone by since my battle with addiction, and life was giving me different and new challenges along the way. Never once had I been satisfied with my current situation. I wanted to get more out of life. I wasn't happy with the same thing over and over again. I wanted more challenges and to learn more stuff as life chugged along.

Most times, I felt like I needed something higher once I attained and successfully accomplished a task. If I chose to stay put, I would simply be staying in my comfort zone. Instead, I chose to challenge myself and further enhance my skills and education to become a fuller person.

But why? Why did I do this? Because soon I started to realize that my life isn't just about myself, but about serving others. This started paving the way for me to find my own purpose and passion in my life.

I'd like to know if you have found your purpose and passion. Why is it that you are on this planet? Who are you? What are you? Who are you becoming? Are your purpose and passion in alignment with your truest essence?

Take a few moments here, and write down the purpose and passion you're seeking out of your life right now.

2nd Level Awakening Without Me Knowing

I was in for a rude awakening in my new position at the auto glass shop. When you're the lowest guy on the totem pole, you get all the grunt work. Although this time I did not have to clean the washroom, I did have to sweep the floors, clean up around the garbage area, assist senior staff members with the dirty work they didn't want to do and do some interior painting in the shop. I didn't mind it, as I knew I had to start somewhere. I realized this is the nature of any workplace, when starting a new position. So, I focused on the positives rather than grumble and complain about it.

During my time with the glass company, I kept injuring myself. It was physical and laborious and required many different sharp tools in order to replace the windshield. The process involved cutting away at the urethane glue, in order for the old windshield to be removed easily. Then, I had to use a scraper to remove any residual glue and clean the surface. Last, I had to prime the surface to allow the new glue to set on top of the new windshield. Most importantly, I had to be very careful not to damage the vehicle's interior while doing all this. One careless slip of the razor and I could scratch the dashboard or the roof liner, which would be very costly.

Like any new job, there was a three-month probationary period. Somehow, I managed to last, though I thought I wouldn't since I'd made numerous mistakes that cost the company. It was very difficult, as I had to learn so many different things in such a short period of time.

The learning curve for this industry was extremely steep. For example, I once made a costly mistake while attempting to lay the urethane glue along the frame for a new windshield. Not only does the urethane hold the windshield in place, it also acts as a barrier to prevent liquids from coming inside the vehicle. Unfortunately, I didn't join the glue properly and it created a small gap. As soon as it rained, the water leaked into the dashboard of the vehicle, ruining the client's radio system. Because I caused the damaged, the company had to replace the radio for the client. I thought I would be fired. Instead, the manager that hired me assigned me to another position, making auto glass deliveries.

This new assignment involved me driving to the distribution warehouse to pick up various glass parts and dropping them off at various destinations throughout town. I didn't mind it, as it took my mind off of my mistakes, got me away from the shop and kept me busy. For a while, I thought I would not last. I was ready to quit and go back to my old job, but that meant admitting defeat and giving up on myself, which I was not about to do.

My Lifetime Partner

I'd been single for about three months and I still had some negative emotions about my last relationship. I knew I had to move on because finding a lasting relationship was very important to me, and I wasn't getting any younger. I wanted to find a girl who shared my dreams and wanted to have kids and grow old together. I started to go out again to meet people and take my mind off of the past.

On the weekends, I would go out clubbing to drink, meet my friends and dance the night away. One night, my friends and I went to a club somewhere around west side of town. I hadn't been to this particular night club before. I wasn't driving, so I had a few drinks. We were on the dance floor, when suddenly I saw her. The most beautiful woman I had ever laid eyes on was dancing up on a stage in front of me. She was captivating and mesmerizing. She captured my heart instantly. I just stood there gazing at her. Time stood still as I kept looking. She had an exotic look that really made her stand out, and made it difficult to pinpoint her ethnicity.

My friends noticed my constant staring at her all night long and they kept telling me to get her phone number. If it wasn't for them encouraging me, I wouldn't have done so because I'm the shy type. But if there was one thing I'd learned throughout the years, it was this: if you want something in life, you have to go get it. So, after some hesitation, I worked up the courage to go up on the stage to introduce myself.

I tapped her on the shoulder and when she turned to look at me, my knees nearly gave out. The music was blaring so loudly it was hard to start a conversation, but I trudged through.

"Uh... hi," I stammered. "I'm Keith. I just wanted to tell you that you're the most beautiful girl I've ever seen. What's your name?" I couldn't believe I was actually speaking to her!

"Thank you," she said. "I'm Helen."

"I don't want to lose this opportunity," I said. "I was wondering if I can have your phone number so we can go out some time. I really want to get to know you better and I don't want to lose this chance, if I don't see you again."

She smiled and then she gave me her phone number! I was so blown away, I felt like I was in heaven.

A few days later, I found the courage to give her a call. It was a pager number she had given me, so I keyed my phone number into the dial pad, indicating for her to call me back. A few hours later she called me and asked who I was. I told her I was the guy she'd met at the club over the weekend. She remembered me and agreed to go out on a date a few days later.

On our first date, I picked her up at her place and we went to a bar for a few drinks. When she got into my car, the first thing that caught my attention was her fragrant perfume that filled the air. When we got to the bar, we spent many hours together just chatting away. She was absolutely stunning, and we clicked right away.

I found out that Helen was half Vietnamese, one-quarter French and one-quarter Chinese, hence why I could not figure out her background. She had a unique blend of different cultures in her blood, which contributed to her exotic look. She was born in Vietnam, but her family had to escape the country, as war was breaking out. So, she came to Montreal when she was only 8. She could speak Vietnamese, English and French, and she worked full-time as a pharmacy technician for a big-chain drug store. Helen was also a single mother, raising a beautiful 3-year-old little girl, Amanda.

As a first-date surprise, I had a nice bouquet of flowers waiting in my car. When I drove her home, I got out of my car and presented them to her. She was so happy, and we gave each other a big hug. I didn't want to come on too strong on our first date.

When my parents found out I had met this wonderful woman, they wanted to meet her, too. I told them about how beautiful, intelligent and funny she was. By then, we'd spoken on the phone many times and gone out on a few dates.

One day, I asked her if she would be interested in coming over for Chinese New Year dinner with my parents. She agreed, though I later found out that she didn't normally go to someone's home so early in a relationship, which made me feel particularly special.

When she came over, I introduced her to my parents. We sat in the living room enjoying our traditional Chinese dinner of sticky rice, shitake mushroom soup, vegetables and fried noodles. My parents really enjoyed her company. They found her to be a positive, upbeat and loving person. The key thing is that she has a beautiful heart.

After only dating for about a month, we decided to move in together. I met her daughter, and it was only a few months into the relationship that she started calling me daddy; I was happy with that.

During the first few months of living together, I must admit it was quite rocky. We were just getting to know each other better and some things didn't align. Because of this, we argued quite a bit. It took some time for us to understand each other, but over time the disagreements lessened. I could tell she was the one for me. I felt it in my heart. I wanted to settle down, get married and have kids with her.

I felt the importance and the need to tell Helen about what kind of life I had endured. As I described the abuse from my dad, the bullying, the gang lifestyle and the drug addiction, she just took it all in. Then, she gave me a big hug and said, "Thank you for sharing your story with me. I don't care about what you've done in the past, as long as you're not doing it now. It's these events that made you who you are."

"Thanks honey," I said, completely blown away by her acceptance of my past. "It means a lot to me to get this off my chest. I need you to know everything about me."

"I appreciate the fact that you told me this," she replied. "I'm with you because of your big heart. I can feel it. That's why I chose you."

When those words came out of her mouth, I kissed her passionately and hugged her for what seemed like an eternity.

At that point, I was longing to get married. I was in my late 20's and I wanted to settle down. When I'd met Helen, it was love at first sight. As I got to know her better, my love for her only grew stronger. It was almost like I'd known her all my life. I guess you could say she was my soul mate. The chemistry was there, and our likes and dislikes were identical: we were both ambitious, we both loved food and cooking and we both loved kids. Only three months into our relationship, I asked her to marry me.

"You know what, honey?" I asked.

"What?" She replied.

"I love you."

"I love you too!"

"I want to grow old with you and have kids with you."

"Really?" She asked. "Me, too."

"So, I've been thinking…"

"What's that hon?"

I could tell she was becoming suspicious.

"I think we should get married," I said. She went silent for a moment and I felt my heart stop, but I had to continue. "Will you marry me?"

She looked over at me for a moment and then gave me one of the most passionate kisses. It seemed to last forever.

"Yes!" She said so happily.

"I love you honey."

Almost immediately afterward, we started planning our wedding. We originally intended on having a big, traditional Chinese wedding but things quickly changed. My grandmother had been in the hospital for some time and was getting worse. I worried that if something bad were to happen to her, we couldn't get married as planned. In the Chinese tradition, it's bad luck to get married within a year of a family member's death.

I asked Helen what we should do. We both agreed it was best to have a smaller wedding in our backyard with some of our closest friends. So, things had to be put together quickly. I needed to find a marriage commissioner and had to pick my Best Man. We were married within the week! It turned out we didn't need all the extravagance of a big wedding. All we needed was the two of us.

Chapter 5: Persistence and Miracles

Another Opportunity Up the Rung

I had always been ambitious and yearned to learn more, but once I met Helen, my motivation to improve my life grew exponentially. This renewed commitment to be true to myself definitely showed in my work. I promised myself there would be no more errors or silly mistakes on my part.

The manager gave me one last opportunity to prove myself. He teamed me up with another glass technician who had been in the industry for over 20 years. He taught me every trick in the book and showed me what to look out for. When it came to very difficult or odd jobs, he was the man assigned by the glass company to solve any challenges. He mentored me and gave all his heart in my training. He even invented a tool and named it after me. He called it The Tonger, and it was used to help chisel out the glue to remove the broken windshield. Thanks to his teachings and wisdom, I quickly climbed up the ladder at the glass company and became a mobile glass technician.

As a mobile glass technician, the company provided me with a van to store my tools and parts in, and to drive to and from work. They also enrolled me in an extended health plan. Helen was so proud of my achievements and how far I'd come. Even my fellow employees were offering many praises and acknowledgments for how much I had improved and changed.

There were times I wanted to quit because the position was difficult and it took a toll on my body. Some of my fellow coworkers even had chronic pain issues, as the position was extremely labor-intensive. Most of them had to file workers' compensation claims for their injuries. Depending on the injury type, one could take up to six weeks off of work to heal.

One time, I was injured so badly that the person who hired me questioned my ability to continue, and I started asking myself the very same question. I wondered how much longer I would survive if I remained in this industry. I didn't want to be like the other guys who had developed long-term issues in their body.

My mentor continued to give me every opportunity to learn new things and he encouraged me to go after what I wanted in life. I am grateful for his wisdom as I chose not to give up on myself and to always continue working on improving my skills. To achieve this, I needed to follow his advice and get out of my comfort zone.

Reflection:

Even though I'd hit rock bottom, I had to start anew and take inventory of all the good things in my life. Oftentimes, I would reflect back and see how much I'd grown. Successfully beating my addiction has been my biggest achievement.

Another major milestone was to quit smoking. I knew how much it was damaging my body. I forget how many times I tried to quit, but it was definitely one difficult habit to break. I was finally able to stop because I had to think of my future and my family's future, as well. Plus, it was starting to become an expensive habit.

Earlier in the book, I asked you to take inventory of your thoughts and beliefs. Well, Nugget Number 6 is to take inventory of your accomplishments. They can be both mental and physical highlights. It could be a promotion, completing a course that helped to increase your knowledge, losing some weight, taking on some healthy habits or acquiring certain assets.

By taking stock of your successes, you will begin to recognize how far you've come. Oftentimes, I look at my own inventory because it reminds me how much I've grown.

So, take some time and think as far back as your childhood. Use this page to start listing them here below. Once that's done, be grateful for all the things that have come to you along the way. Learn to love and appreciate where you are in life because living is the most precious gift of all.

The Newest Addition to My Family

One day, Helen and I were invited to a friend's birthday party. We had a few drinks and we were dancing the night away, when suddenly we had to leave because Helen wasn't feeling well. When we got home, she ran to the bathroom and vomited.

The next morning, Helen decided to take a pregnancy test. Something inside of her just told her to do so. All of a sudden, she came running out of the washroom jumping up and down, saying she was pregnant. I was in the kitchen preparing breakfast for us and the next thing I knew, I was jumping up and down with her. I grabbed her and picked her up, embracing in our love for each other and what we were about to embark on together.

During the entire pregnancy, there were moments when Helen was extremely nauseous. Other times she was having weird cravings for junk food. One minute she'd want a burger and the next minute she'd want something very sour. Luckily, my parents were helping out with our daughter, Amanda. They would take her to daycare and bring her back home. Sometimes, we would even go to my parents' house to eat dinner because we were too busy to cook at home.

Before we had decided to have a baby, Helen wanted me to have some blood test to make sure our genetics were compatible. Thankfully, they were. We'd also decided to hold off on revealing the sex of our baby because we both wanted the suspense of surprise. Both Helen and I really wanted a boy since we already had a girl, and we thought it would be nice for Amanda to have a baby brother.

At times, Helen would be sitting on the couch and then suddenly our baby would be boxing inside of her stomach. I would press my hands gently on her tummy to feel the sensation. I was so fascinated with how life could grow inside of Helen. It brought tears to my eyes to think about how much I'd gone through, how many near-death experiences I'd had, and still I had the ability to create a life with my loved one. I thanked God for giving me so many chances in life.

In the last trimester of Helen's pregnancy, the ultrasounds showed that everything was okay. But as the due date approached, Helen's sickness became more frequent and even worsened. When she started to have pain in her stomach, we went back to the doctor to make sure things were fine.

After another round of ultrasounds, we learned that our baby was in a breech position. The doctor said there was still some time and that maybe the baby would flip on its own. She suggested we do some massaging along the stomach area, hoping it would flip. However, this method didn't help at all. In fact, the massage proved to be extremely painful for Helen. After some more attempts, the doctor stopped and suggested we wait; sometimes the baby would just flip on its own as the due date nears.

I was out on a job site one day, working in a body shop with my mentor, when I got a call from Helen. She was in extreme pain and needed to go to the hospital right away.

"Hey Keith," she said when I answered the phone. "I need to go to the hospital. I'm in a lot of pain."

I could hear the fear in her voice, and I was very concerned. "Is it hurting that much?" I asked.

"Yes, I need to go *now*," she said.

"Okay, let me call my boss and I'll be right there."

I called my boss immediately to explain the situation, and he told me to go at once. I picked up Helen at home and drove straight to the emergency room at the BC Women's Hospital. The nurses took her in to do a quick analysis. Our baby wanted out three weeks ahead of the due date. Unfortunately, our baby had not yet flipped, so Helen had to go in for an emergency c-section surgery. Everything happened so fast.

I went into the emergency room with Helen and she was under some heavy anesthesia. I couldn't see much because I was behind a curtain. Time seemed to pass like an eternity. But before I knew it, the doctor was asking me if I wanted to cut the umbilical cord. It was all bloody and sort of freaked me out. I declined, as I had already nearly fainted from what I had seen when I peeped over the curtain.

It was a boy.

It took some time for him to cry for air and I was starting to get a little nervous. The seconds passed like minutes, while I wondered if he was fine. Then, our baby was crying loudly as he gasped for his first breath in an unknown world. I was so relieved to hear him cry out loud.

When I looked at Helen, I saw tears rolling down her cheeks. The nurses guided our baby toward us for a quick glimpse before they took him away for observations. It's common procedure for the nurses to take the baby for additional testing to make sure everything is okay.

The doctor said our baby was jaundice and needed to be put under special lights. They took him straight to another section of the hospital to treat his jaundice skin condition. The doctor said we wouldn't be able to see him for another day, and Helen was escorted to another room where she would stay for the next five days.

I called my parents and my boss to tell them the good news. I was allowed to stay at the hospital for the next few days, so I took some time off work to take care of Helen and our newborn son. The hospital staff brought me some cushions, so that I could have a place to sleep. We asked my parents to take care of Amanda while Helen and I were in the hospital.

Later on, the nurses told us that our son needed to stay for a few more hours of additional treatment. There was water in his lungs and they confirmed he was jaundice. They wanted him to connect with his mother soon, so she could begin breastfeeding him. While we were in the hospital room, we thought about what to name our son. After going back and forth for a few days, we decided to name him Jacob.

On our third day at the hospital, I picked up Amanda from my parents' house, so she could see her mom and meet her new brother. She was excited and happy. After seeing and hugging mommy, I took her to find her brother, Jacob. This would be my second opportunity to see him since the surgery. We proceeded down the halls to find where he was. There were so many babies in the room. After looking around, we found him. He was beautiful and sleeping soundly in his bed.

A day later, the nurses brought Jacob in to get Helen acquainted with him. The nurse took Jacob and placed him right beside her. We were both happy to see him. Immediately, the nurses assisted Helen with getting Jacob to latch onto her breast, so that he may begin feeding. It took many attempts, but soon nature set in and Helen and Jacob were beautifully bonded.

Helen was still in pain from the operation and only time would heal her from the surgery. After about five days we were able to go home. We finally took Jacob to his new house.

Reflection:

Being able to create a life with my loved one, my soul mate, is the greatest gift I could've received during this period of my life. From lifting myself out of a deep hole, filled with hopelessness and helplessness, to being able to create a life in just nine months, is a miracle. Words cannot describe my feelings and emotions.

When that moment happened, something filled my heart. It felt like a surge of energy filled my entire body and gave me the strength, purpose and motivation to do better in life. I was motivated to provide all the abundance in the world, and a better life for my family. I am forever grateful to the universe for giving me a chance in life and to be able to give back in whatever way I can.

I love my life!

Getting Out of My Comfort Zone

I had been working for the glass company for close to five years, and things were going well, except for the times I injured myself. If it wasn't my elbow, there were cuts around my fingers.

One day, Amanda asked me, "Daddy, if you are always hurting yourself, why don't you just change jobs?" Her question hit me like a ton of bricks. I couldn't believe that a six-year-old could give me such insight into my life.

Occasionally, I would still communicate with Grant, my former boss from the oil change company. Sometimes, he would ask if I wanted to come back to work for him because he missed me. I knew the company had changed hands. The previous owner had decided to retire, so he sold his chain of stores to a big U.S. chain that was moving into Canada.

One day, Grant, pulled me aside and asked if I would be interested in working for a quick lube supply company that was gaining a presence in the British Columbia marketplace. The company was headquartered in Ontario and they were expanding into the western region of Canada, mainly Alberta and BC. They had two distribution centers, one in Ontario and one in Alberta.

"Hey Keith," Grant began. "How's it going lately?"

"Not too bad," I replied. "Things are pretty good. How have you been?"

"Not too shabby. Hey, just wanted to know if you're looking for another opportunity? How's your current place treating you?"

"I haven't really thought about it," I said, honestly. "I have my own van and things are good for me. I have my family now so that's my focus. What kind of opportunity is this, by the way?"

"There's a company from Ontario looking to come to BC, and they need a sales rep to look after the BC location. I think this could be a right fit for you."

"Thanks Grant," I said. "That means a lot to me. But for now, I'm happy where I'm at. I'm working for a big company and I have benefits for my family. That's important to me, so I think I'll pass on this one."

"I understand. Think about it anyway, okay? I don't want you turning down an opportunity like this, Keith."

"Sure, Grant. Let me go home and talk about it with my wife. I appreciate you reaching out to me, bud."

That night, I talked to Helen about the opportunity and how I wanted to wave it off. She whacked me on the side of my head and told me I was crazy not to find out more information. She said I should never turn down any opportunity without going deeper into the process.

Just before going to bed that night, I began asking questions about who I am and what kind of future I want for myself and my family. I already knew that I couldn't stay in my current position for the next ten years because it was so hard on my body. Plus, I knew there wasn't much room for advancement either.

The next day, I called Grant and told him I wanted to revisit the opportunity. I acknowledge it was silly of me to not listen to the full story and get all the facts on the opportunity.

"Hey Grant," I said when he answered. "Is this a good time to talk?"
"Yeah sure, what's up?" He asked.

"You know Grant, I told Helen about our conversation and she smacked me right on my head." I heard him laughing on the other end of the phone. "Yeah, yeah, yeah," I continued, feeling foolish. "Grant, could you please arrange for an appointment so I could sit down for an interview regarding this opportunity."

"Okay," he said, still chuckling. "I'll see what I can do."

"Oh, and Grant?"

"Yeah?"

"Thanks for bringing this opportunity to me. I owe you one, buddy."

"Anytime, bud. That's what I'm here for."

I did not tell any of my co-workers about my interview or this opportunity. It was going to be a fact-finding session more than anything else.

During the interview process, I was greeted by one of the owners of the company, Mike. I met him at a local quick lube center, which was already a client of theirs. He asked me all sorts of questions such as how long I'd been involved in the automotive industry and what motivated me to stay in it. I could tell by his body movements that he was impressed by the way I answered his questions. After that session, he proceeded to tell me what the position involved.

The opening was for an accounts manager in the BC region and it involved visiting all the quick lube stores to promote their products and services. It would require going out of town for several days at a time to manage the accounts, depending on where they were located. BC was the only province that didn't have much market share, so the accounts manager would be responsible for generating new clients in the BC market.

As the session progressed, I learned there were about 50 stores in the BC region that specialized in the quick lube industry and they predicted that number to increase to 75 - 85 by the end of five years. I was very excited once I heard what the position was all about and what the perks would be. The company paid well, they would give me a car allowance and I would be classified as a sub-contractor, which meant I would be self-employed. It had been one of my dreams to have my very own business. This would be the perfect opportunity for me and my family.

A month later, I received an email from another owner of the company announcing that I would be part of their team. Helen and I jumped up and down in celebration. I told Amanda that I had taken her advice and found another job so that I would no longer be hurting myself. She was proud of me for taking her advice.

Chapter 6: Growth and Confidence

A Taste of Being Self-Employed

Once I knew the starting date for my new position, I gave my two weeks' notice to my current employer. The new company wanted me to start right away, which involved me flying to Toronto for extensive training on their products and services.

I was in Toronto for about 10 days to learn the ins and outs of the products and services they offered. From there, I teamed up with one of their current representatives that was already looking after the BC market. He was managing Alberta, Saskatchewan and parts of Winnipeg. Hence, why they wanted somebody in the BC region. All the years of learning and training on my own in sales and in the network marketing industry had finally paid off. I could finally apply what I had learned.

One of the company's requirements was to have a reliable car. Therefore, my car needed to be changed, as it was over twenty years old and would not be safe enough to travel long distances.

Because I was now self-employed, I turned one of the rooms in our home into an office. Soon after coming back from my training in Ontario, there was a big truck parked outside of our home. It delivered a pallet filled with literature and sample products for me to give away to potential candidates needing my offerings. The pallet was about four feet high and filled with all sorts of goodies.

The position I'd taken on required another level of learning. I had to make decisions and choices that would be in the best interest of the company and I had to keep the customers satisfied. I had to put my sales experience to the test. I met a lot of business owners from different backgrounds and walks of life. Some had no idea about the workings of the quick lube industry, while others had prior experience running a quick lube.

During my travels and meetings with these owners, I often needed to adjust my sales techniques when trying to promote a service or product. Certain techniques that worked with owner A, didn't work with owner B. I soon realized that I did not know everything and I needed to upgrade my sales techniques and approach. I needed to learn more and improve my techniques, as I was hitting many walls with various clients. It was a year into my contract with the company and I knew I needed to upgrade my knowledge in order to gain more sales. But instead, I just rode it out, hoping my experience would be enough for me to gain what I needed to improve my performance.

In the second year of this new experience, I learned the hard way how important it was to deliver products and services without offending anyone. One day, the son of a renowned franchise business owner called my boss to complain about me. He said he did not agree with my sales technique and that from then on, I was not allowed to step foot in his store.

When my boss approached me, I was taken aback by the news. It made me feel unsure of myself, and I was afraid I would lose my job. This client was extremely important to the company I was representing. I began to question my own skills and came to the conclusion that I needed to learn more.

By this time, my son was about a year and half. Thankfully, my parents were helping Helen and me take care of the kids so that Helen could begin working again. She landed a sales job that required her to travel around the province just like me, but instead of being in the automotive industry, Helen was in the pharmaceutical industry. She had been in the industry for over fifteen years.

One day, I came across an ad in the newspaper that caught my attention. It was all about having the opportunity to make more money by developing the mind-set of a millionaire. That was enough to peak my interest and make me look into it further. To top it off, the event was free to attend, so it was a no brainer. *What is there to lose, besides my time*, I asked myself.

I spoke to Helen about the opportunity and we both agreed we should check it out. That evening we attended the event. The speaker explained what a money blueprint was and how it can always be adjusted. He said that everyone has, what he called, a "financial thermostat." He went on to say that most people's financial thermostat is set too low, which means their beliefs about money may be limiting and/or limited. Most of these beliefs have been sub-programmed into our minds since childhood by our family, peers and environment. Who we choose to hang out with can also have an effect on our money beliefs. He also discussed the challenges everyone faces when money problems show up in our lives and how attending this event could be life-changing, simply by finding out what our money thermostat is set at.

As the evening progressed, I noticed some people getting up and leaving the room. Everything the speaker said resonated within me, in a very deep way. One key point I took away was the idea that my current financial situation was why I may not be increasing my wealth. He went on to say that the programing I received as a child could be holding me back. He invited us for a three-day intensive training program where he would look at our financial blueprint and analyze the causes that were keeping us from making more money.

Towards the end of the event, I thought the speaker was going to try to sell something to the audience. Instead, he gave an irresistible offer I couldn't believe. He went on to explain that the three-day course was valued at almost $2,000 per person. He then started slashing the price down. First to 75% of the regular cost, then 50% and finally down to 25%. I was ready to get up and go to the back of the room to sign up, when suddenly, he slashed the remaining 25% completely and said everyone in the room gets to attend this amazing three-day event for *free*! Helen and I looked at each other and smiled. We couldn't believe it. *Is there something missing here*? *What's the catch*? The speaker said there was no catch, whatsoever. So, Helen and I signed up that night.

It was a few weeks before we were able to attend the event. I had arranged for my parents to look after both of the kids, as the event lasted from morning until late into the evening.

On our first morning, there were hundreds of people packed into a large meeting room that was located in a prestigious downtown hotel. I was blown away by the amount of content that was covered on our first day. The speaker for this three-day intensive was T. Harv Eker. He wrote the book, *The Secrets of a Millionaire Mind*, which became a #1 best seller. He stated, "Give me five minutes, and I can predict your financial blueprint for the rest of your life!"

When the first day was over, I realized my financial blueprint, which consists of the money and success blueprint, was set very low. In order for me to increase my wealth and financial blueprint, and to achieve the level of success I wanted, I needed to set my financial thermostat higher. The financial thermostat is the relationship between a person's comfort level and their level of wealth. It's not only indicative of how much money I have in my bank account, but is more largely dependent on my subconscious beliefs about money and wealth. The lower my financial thermostat was set, the harder it would be for me to build and keep my wealth.

My financial thermostat needed to be much higher than it was, and I needed to change many of my limited beliefs about money. For example, I had the beliefs that money is hard to make, that it's easy to spend and lose money, that I don't deserve a lot of money and that money is only for smart people. I also learned a lot about myself and how my childhood was a contributing factor to my financial status. I needed to let go of the past and make the necessary adjustments, physically, mentally and spiritually, to take myself to a whole new level.

Helen and I cried and laughed throughout those three days. All the sharing we did was extremely helpful, as it paved the way for us to become business partners later on in life.

During the whole three-day event, they were upselling all sorts of programs. It began to make sense, as I was wondering how they could afford to host a seminar like this without charging people. There were a variety of programs I thought would benefit me and I wanted to pursue. The only program I could afford was called Train the Trainer. The program was valued just under $5,000, but they did another irresistible offer of only $2,995. I really needed help with my sales position, so I took the leap and bought the program.

The training for Train the Trainer would take place a few months later, and consisted of five full days of learning for me. Now, these days were very intense, as training started at 9:00am sharp and ended around 11:00pm. One night, we didn't finish until 2:00am and we still had to be back at 9:00am sharp. There was a tremendous amount of information to absorb during those five days.

After finishing the program, and applying the principles I'd learned, I noticed a big change in myself and how I was able to deliver my message and knowledge to my clients. Even my customers and close friends noticed it. I was happier and more confident. The way I was talking, walking and acting displayed a sense of increased self-confidence and motivation.

One expertise I already had was my ability to provide training to my clients. All of my previous experience and hands-on ability had given me the upper hand. One thing that made the company grow so much was the fact that it offered product training for free, allowing business owners to increase their bottom line.

Many business owners complimented me on my Train the Trainer techniques, such as offerings, asking engaging questions and having my clients' employees participate in the learning process. I asked for participation and encouraged raised hands. It wasn't just listening, I made it very experiential for them, as well. This made the training more intriguing and entertaining so the session seemed to go by very quickly, even though it would take at least two full hours. Because all of the business owners saw results so quickly, some of them called my boss and complimented my training abilities. I appreciated their feedback, as it made me feel good.

Within a year of those training sessions, Helen and I had almost doubled our family income. It was amazing. By being open to change and always learning new things, I was able to get myself to the level in life I wanted to be in. I went to various workshops with my arms and mind wide open. With the training I received, I was able to adapt my work habits so that I could fulfill the needs of my clients. I really grew to appreciate all the improvements I'd made in helping my clients achieve success in their business.

As accounts manager, I worked long hours, but I also had flexibility in my schedule, so I was able to pick my kids up and drop them off at school. Having the opportunity to be there for my kids was very important to me and I felt proud of it. When I needed to be out of town, either my parents or Helen would be there for the kids, which is another thing I was grateful for.

My accounts in BC grew substantially. So much that my bosses sat me down one day, when they flew in from Toronto, and suggested opening a distribution center in BC. However, in order to warrant a new distribution center, I needed to increase sales by another 30%. After six months of working and pounding the pavement hard, I had generated enough accounts to open the distribution center in BC. I had increased our thirty accounts to well over a hundred, which was more than I expected to do. In BC alone, we had sales of over $1,000,000.

I was very proud of my achievement, but I cannot take all the credit. It was the warehouse manager, my bosses and the customer service representative working together as a team that made it happen. There were growing pains, but we were able to fix what wasn't working. We adapted, took corrective measures to ensure it didn't happen again and sought to constantly improve. The most important thing was to make sure the wheels kept turning.

As the company kept growing and expanding, internal changes were needed. I realized that once any company hits a certain plateau, it might need additional assistance from outside sources to take it to another level. I'd been with the company for about eight years when one day, the company flew all the sales representatives to Toronto for a meeting. I was wondering what was happening, as this meeting was sort of short notice.

When I sat down in their boardroom with the rest of the sales force, the owners announced that they needed to merge with a large American company that would give them the ability to get the company to the next level. Within six short months, the merger was completed, and there had to be some changes on my end. I could no longer be a sub-contractor, meaning I had to become an employee with the company, instead. This didn't bother me one bit because Helen and I had accumulated enough assets to be able to become real estate investors.

Even though I was no longer a subcontractor with the title of self-employed, I was a real estate investor. I was still self-employed, just in a different field. Helen and I spent thousands of dollars and countless hours looking into the real estate market in our free time so we could increase our wealth. This was something that was taught to us when we attended the three-day, live intensive training years before. The housing market was booming and we ended up investing in two rental properties, generating positive cash flow. We created a corporation so that we could have the properties underneath the company for tax purposes and business write-offs.

It had been close to 10 years of me being a sales representative for the automotive company and Helen working as a sales rep for a pharmaceutical company. We had many conversations about what it would be like to really have our own business. Yes, we were generating pretty good income, but we wanted something for ourselves. Both of us felt like we were ready for a life of entrepreneurship, becoming our own bosses and making our dreams come true. We wanted time, freedom and financial independence. We wanted to give back to the community, while building a nest egg for our kids.

Reflection:

Nugget Number 7 for the reader is this: Always be open and always be learning. There's a famous saying that states, "The day I stop learning will be the day I start dying." I don't want to be that kind of person. In order to ensure that doesn't happen, I had to get out of my comfort zone.

In order for real change to happen, there has to be enough pain for us to *want* to change. Oftentimes, most people will go back to their comfort zone and remain the same. Nothing will happen until you step out of your comfort zone.

Another obstacle that inhibits people from getting out of their comfort zone is uncertainty. Most people don't like living this way, as they don't know what tomorrow will be like for them. It's no longer predictable nor in their control. They are not ready to let go and allow whatever happens to happen. But this is a natural process of evolution.

Successful people are action takers and doers. They take risks in order to attain what they want in life. So, have an open mind to whatever possibilities are out there for you. If you always remain the same, nothing will change. The definition of insanity is doing the same thing over and over again and expecting different results - that will never happen.

So, my question for the reader is, are you living in your comfort zone? Or are you going through the pain of uncertainty, knowing it's something you must do to attain your dreams, goals and aspirations?

Write down what it is that's holding you back. Or, write down what you are attaining and wishing to see in your life.

Real Entrepreneurship

One drawback of our work as sales representatives was the fact that both Helen and I had to go out of town often. Some months we would only see our kids two out of the four weeks. We realized we needed a change, so that we could spend more time with the kids as they started getting older. We were also getting tired of traveling around, sleeping in hotels and eating out all the time. I was gaining quite a bit of weight and getting a little chunky on my sides.

During the winter, it was dangerous driving across the roads, due to snow and fog. There were many times I would be driving with white knuckles on both hands. Some destinations took as much as 10 hours of driving to get to. One time, while I was driving through a mountain pass, it was snowing very heavily. Suddenly, I felt a slip of the car. I lost control of the vehicle and slid into a ditch. If the car had veered off in the other direction, I would've driven off the cliff. It was a scary event. From that point on, I resented having to drive in the snow. One lesson I learned, however, was to never go cheap on snow tires. My life is worth way more than the couple hundred bucks of savings.

At that time, we bought our very first place: a tri-level, three-bedroom townhouse. It needed a lot of work, so we hired a friend to help us do some renovations and we moved in a few days later. I was so proud that Helen and I were able to buy our very first home.

Helen and I were always on the lookout for new opportunities. One thing we learned was that when an opportunity presented itself, we needed to be able to take action right away. Helen and I knew that we were both doers, willing and ready to take action.

There were many discussions where Helen would constantly tell me how lucrative the pharmacy business was. She knew the ins and outs of the industry, so I trusted her judgment. There was a little old Vietnamese lady that owned a pharmacy in East Vancouver who was contemplating retirement. Helen knew her well and had become quite fond her, as she had been a client for a number of years. Helen thought it would be a good idea for both of us to pursue this opportunity.

When the time came, Helen introduced me to the woman and her husband. The lady asked if we were serious about buying her pharmacy. It was a community pharmacy servicing the local area. She wasn't always able to be at the store, and if the patients needed their medication, they would have to call her ahead of time to set up an appointment.

We did some diligent research, like going to city hall to look at the kinds of people living in the area, nearby clinics and competitors. Once we were satisfied, Helen and I knew it would be a good opportunity with this location so we made an offer. The lady accepted and we proceeded with the process of buying our first business. Of course, we hired a lawyer to make sure all our bases were covered.

Right away, we were faced with two challenges. First, to own a pharmacy, a majority of the shareholders needed to have a valid pharmacists license. Second, we needed to find about $250,000 to purchase the business. These were not easy challenges, but through Helen's contacts and our perseverance we were able to complete the transaction.

We found a business partner who was a pharmacist that was interested, so the first challenge was met with success. The second challenge of coming up with the $250K was difficult and arduous, to say the least. This was in 2008, the same year there was worldwide financial meltdown, which meant it was an extremely grueling time to get money from a bank, unless you had a sound business proposal to present to them. I spent countless hours researching what it took to create a sound business proposal, so we could obtain financing.

After one full week, I managed to have all the numbers and the projections required for the first five years. In the business plan, I indicated who the executives of the business were and how we would manage to grow the opportunity. We went to three financial institutions with no success. One of those was even a B lender, but still no success. As the deadline was quickly approaching, we needed to find a solution soon. I told Helen that even if we didn't succeed, at least we could be confident that we had tried everything possible and, more importantly, it would have been a good learning experience for us.

Both of us went in to apply for a loan one last time with another financial institute. If this didn't work, our next plan would be to ask if the seller would be willing to accept a vendor take-back mortgage, but that meant she would still have control of the company. I wasn't too enthusiastic with this option, as I knew that she had another party interested, if our deal fell through.

The stakes were high. Helen, our business partner and I sat down with the lender of this bank and presented our business plan to her. The department we sought financing through specialized in healthcare, specifically. The lender took all the necessary information and documents and said she would have news for us in a few days. A few days later, I received a phone call from the lender informing us that we had been approved. We got the full $250K to seal the deal. That's 100% financing with no money down. We couldn't believe it. I was so grateful for this opportunity and thanked the universe for allowing me to move on to the next chapter in life. Our first pharmacy was called Viet Pharmacy Remedy's Rx.

From then on, things rolled along pretty smoothly with the transitions. There were still some additional challenges along the way. We had to do a bit of renovations to get the store presentable for our patients, as it was a bit worn and dilapidated.

For the next two years, while Helen was running our business, I was still working as accounts manager for the automotive company. I couldn't quit my job until our business started generating some real profits, and Helen had to take a huge pay cut to keep the business afloat for the first two years. We knew that to get to the next level it meant we had to walk two steps back in order to walk three steps forward.

Also, the agreement with our business partner didn't quite work out as anticipated. He was running around between three different companies, so he was always showing up late and wasn't performing 100% to his ability. We ended up hiring a part-time pharmacist to help fill the days our partner was unable to work.

Those two years were extremely difficult for us to juggle family and our finances. Helen would come home around 9:00pm because there was just so much to do at the pharmacy. There was paperwork, counting pills and managing our inventory. We had to be able to manage our inventory carefully or else it would eat into the profit and limit our cash flow.

There were times Helen and I had to work on Sundays, attending various networking events to raise awareness for our business. As for the finance part, we had bills and a mortgage to manage. After our second year in the business, things started to turn around. Helen and I were able to terminate the original agreement we had with our business partner, meaning we had 100% ownership of the company. Within six months of the two-year mark, I resigned from my position as accounts manager to help with the business.

Being your own boss brings a whole new dimension and experience to life. There was so much I needed to do. If I didn't manage all the day to day operations, things would fall behind. Helen and I made great business partners because we each knew what we needed to do. While she was running the pharmacy business on the front end, I would handle the back-end projects, such as marketing and promoting the brand.

We soon realized, that just because there was an open sign on the door, it didn't mean customers would come in. We needed to raise awareness among the public and bring in new customers. I went to many networking events and knocked door-to-door doing marketing and advertising for our business in the local community. Some people in the area didn't even know there was a community pharmacy nearby, let alone that the pharmacy had been there for a decade. I realized that becoming an entrepreneur comes with lots of work, responsibility and dedication.

The Second Store

After the third year, things were coming along nicely. We increased the number of staff members and had to hire a part-time bookkeeper to make sure everything was in order. I felt it was time to open another store, so I started looking around in the Lower Mainland. I thought Burnaby would be a good area, so I asked Helen what she thought. She agreed with Burnaby Heights because there were many doctors in that area, but not many pharmacies, especially not one with a community-like setting.

One particular location caught my eye. It was a complex with retail space on the bottom floor and residential space on the upper floors. After some time, I managed to find the landlord and I gave him a call to introduce myself. I told him that I was interested in renting a spot when one became available. He told me nothing would be available in the near future, but he would consider me when the time came.

A few months later, the landlord contacted me and told me a property was available. So, we got the lease paperwork prepared for our 2nd location. But this time, it would be a whole new learning experience. Buying an existing store, like we had done originally, was an excellent opportunity. But those were really hard to find. This second property would be a whole new start up for us. It meant having to deal with the city, the planning department, getting approval with the BC College of Pharmacists and dealing with contractors. It was hard work and a steep learning curve, but extremely rewarding. Before the year was over, we opened our second location: Northburn Remedy's Rx.

Within one year of running our second location, Helen and I were presented with another opportunity: a store located within a five-minute drive from our original store. It was nice, but it needed renovations. Helen suggested that this location was big enough to include a walk-in medical clinic tied in to the pharmacy. I thought that was a great idea, but we didn't have any experience in that area, and the price tag on this pharmacy was substantially higher that the first one. However, we didn't allow ourselves be intimidated by these new challenges. We knew we just needed to find a way to purchase this store.

This time, we approached a bank we had been dealing with on a personal level. We had been working with several banks between our two stores and wanted to streamline everything into one. Fortunately for us, we found a contact in the bank's healthcare department. The bank wanted all of our business, so they worked with us to guarantee a win-win situation. Within a few weeks of our initial meeting with them, they approved us for a loan. Again, we managed to secure 100% financing. The person who handled the loan was very surprised, as it's not common to qualify for financing without some sort of down-payment.

Our vision for the third store was to have one-third of the space as a pharmacy and the rest as a medical clinic for doctors to serve patients in the community. Dealing with the city of Vancouver was very time consuming. I didn't have the time to do all the running around, so I hired a contractor to assist us with the store. It was harder to deal with the city of Vancouver than it was to deal with the city of Burnaby. The city of Vancouver had far more restrictions and by-laws, regarding pharmacy stores.

Once the space was renovated, we called our third store Main Street Remedy's Rx. Though the newly renovated pharmacy was running smoothly, we still had another challenge: finding doctors to move into the clinic. Finding doctors is like finding a needle in a haystack. We had a few potential doctors interested in the space, but nothing transpired. We came so close to signing a lease with a group of doctors, but that party got cold feet and backed out. The clinic sat empty for over a year and things took a turn for the worse in no time.

Chapter 7: Life and Loss in Business

Years of Hard Work Crashing Down

Just when we thought things were moving along smoothly, we were audited by a governing agency in our seventh year of the pharmacy business. Two of our three stores specialized in mental health and addiction services, for which we billed the governing body on a regular basis. A team of auditors came into these stores and checked our paperwork to see if things were in order. They spent nearly a week in each store. Once they were done, we did not hear from them for nearly a year and a half.

During that time, I had also opened up a local coffee shop, but it was proving to be a serious mistake, as we already had so much on our plate. The renovations for the third pharmacy had gone way over budget. It was expensive to hire contractors and consultants, and the cost put us heavily in debt. I had to plead with the bank to give us additional funding. They ended up granting us a loan increase, but they were not happy about it. If the bank didn't pull through, the contractor was going to put a lien on the store. Having the bankers, the contractors and myself all at the site together wasn't a pleasant experience for any parties involved.

Two years after they initially visited us, the auditors finally came back with their results. They said we owed the governing agency about half a million dollars for discrepancies and errors on our part. They claimed that many of our prescriptions were missing information, such as birthdates, patients' signatures and the date of the prescriptions. These were simply honest administrative mistakes. The majority of pharmacists out there are focused on patient care, and not always administration savvy. The auditors gave us 21 days to submit our arguments. If nothing would be settled, then the government wanted payment immediately.

How could we possibly come up with $500,000 that fast? We contested their findings to make sure that what they had found was legal and that they had just cause. Because of these clerical errors, the government would not honor the prescriptions we billed them for, and they were entitled to receive back the money they had paid.

What we thought to be unfair was the extrapolation calculation they used to reach their conclusion. How they determined their calculation was based on the number of errors. For instance, let's say 25% of the prescriptions we billed them for had errors; they would take the average dollar amount and multiply it by the *total* number of prescriptions we did that year. This is how they got to that huge figure. We didn't have the amount required to pay them and we wanted to challenge them on the basis of their extrapolation process. Helen and I decided the only option would be to take legal action against the governing body.

For Helen and I, as entrepreneurs and community leaders, it was important to help our patients by creating lasting relationships with them, our employees and our local community. As owners of the companies, we made sure all of our employees adhered to the strictest conduct and work ethics. The pharmacists we hired made sure the medications were dispensed correctly and in a timely manner.

Our three stores did upwards of a thousand prescriptions per day. We staffed over forty people and we had a yearly revenue of almost five million dollars. Certainly, mistakes had been made when certain data was missing on the prescriptions. As owners of the company, we owned up to those errors and ensured our employees would not make the same mistakes. We took the necessary precautions, which meant creating another level of protocols and hiring more personnel to do our own self-auditing. As owners, we were responsible for every action our employees took. If an employee made a mistake, then we, the owners, made the mistake as well. This was very difficult for me to swallow because these errors cost us about $500,000.

Our court case with the government turned into a long-drawn-out battle that drained our resources. The entire process took nearly a year, going back and forth between their lawyers and ours. We had to argue with the government lawyers in front of a judge, just to grant us a case to fight the extrapolation. If he allowed it, this would grant us another court date. The judge said we had a good point, so he granted us the extension.

While waiting for the court hearing to be set, I really thought we were going to have to file for bankruptcy, and the mere thought of it brought shivers to my body. While the court battle was taking place, the government started withholding all of our earnings, strangling our cash flow, which was essential to keep our business running. All the money they kept was used to start paying towards the $500K debt. We ended up selling our townhouse in Burnaby, as we needed additional capital to keep the business afloat while we inched closer to our court hearing.

When the governing body learned about the hearing, they wanted to settle with us because under the Pharmaceutical Service Act of BC there was no mention of anything about extrapolation. If we'd won, it would've opened up a huge can of worms. So, they negotiated a reduction of the fee by 50%, bringing it down to $250K, which we thought was a win for us. They mentioned that if we didn't settle and proceeded with the case, the opposing party would go back to our stores and re-do the entire audit process again, even if it took them a whole year. Our lawyers thought that we should take the deal. In the end, neither of us wanted to go to court any longer, so we settled out of court, resulting in what appeared to be a win-win situation.

This event taught us a lot of things about being entrepreneurs. Helen and I were heavily in debt because of the expenses from the renovations and the lawyer fees. This meant running our business a lot leaner by cutting waste, looking at our cash flow, running projections and renegotiating our terms with some of our suppliers.

Sadly, the $250K debt resulted in many cutbacks, and we even had to lay some people off. There were many times I was extremely worried we wouldn't be able to pay our remaining staff members on time. This was a huge responsibility for me because our employees relied on us to put food on their table and to pay rent. I knew many of my employees lived paycheck to paycheck because they were living in one of the most expensive cities in the world. But we needed to keep the business afloat and there were sacrifices to be made. We did what we needed to do to save the company.

The Universe Guiding Us

All of the complications with the government had Helen and I seriously contemplating getting out of the pharmacy business, but we didn't know where to start. We thought about selling our third store so that we could start to simplify our life and have time for ourselves. It had gotten to the point where we often discussed business during dinner with our kids, which is not healthy. It felt like I no longer had quality time with my family. My kids were growing up and I wanted to make sure I'd be spending time with them before they got any older.

While all this was happening, there were times I became negative and resentful toward the world. I was blaming Helen and myself and questioning my beliefs and abilities. At a loss for what to do next, I turned to the universe for a solution. I had a temple at home where I would pray every morning, thanking my gods for everything I was given and asking for support and guidance.

One day, I came across a Facebook ad, marketing a three-day intensive program that was coming to Vancouver. It had been almost ten years since Helen and I had taken the program. I recall looking back at how much I had grown and how that program had changed my life completely. We both knew we had grown leaps and bounds during those ten years, and the current struggles we were having reminded us what was really important in life.

The following week, Helen and I attended the program. The company was called New Peaks, and they offered programs like Never Work Again, Guerilla Business School, Warrior Camp, Wizard Camp, The Greatest Marketing Seminar and Ultimate Relationship Retreat. I attended all the camps while Helen did the Guerilla Business School seminar. We attended The Greatest Marketing Seminar and the Ultimate Relationship Retreat together.

Both the Warrior Camp and Wizard Camp changed my perspective and outlook on life, especially with the recent challenges regarding our pharmacies. Attending those camps had been, by far, the best experiential training I ever acquired. Both camps provided tools I could use to see what's really important in life and how I could face challenges without creating additional chaos in my life.

Helen had to fly to Los Angeles to attend Guerilla Business School. I stayed behind because I needed to take care of the family and the businesses. It was a four-day event, teaching all the different avenues to generate wealth. There were many guest speakers on topics from buying stocks to creating membership sites. However, there was one guest speaker from Vancouver, Colin Sprake, the founder of Make Your Mark, that really stood out to Helen. After listening to him on stage for about 45 minutes, she signed up for his program. His message really resonated with her and she knew we needed someone local to guide and coach us through the difficult times we were facing.

After a few conference calls with Helen and having an opportunity to meet Colin in person at another venue in Vancouver, we signed up for his two-year program, The Business Sherpa Elite. The program was specifically designed for business owners who want to take their business to a whole new level. He talked to Helen and I about what sort of mindset we needed to be in to be successful business owners, which was an extremely important component because the universe will surely throw challenges along the way. Our battle with the opposing party was one of those challenges.

My experience battling it out with the government brought many dark moments for me because I didn't know what the future would hold for me and my family. I was so used to being in control and knowing what tomorrow will be for me. I started feeling down, angry, depressed and playing the victim. I constantly asked myself, *why me? Why* us? To help escape and numb those negative feelings, I would find myself with a Jack Daniels in my left hand and a Johnny Walker in my right. They were my best friends then, but I would pay the dear price the next day.

I had been free of my heroin addiction for almost three decades, only my family, my wife and a few close friends knew what had happened to me earlier in my life. To be totally honest, I thought I had healed myself completely until I started working on my inner world.

As part of my healing journey, it was important for me to resolve what had been hidden and unresolved. There'd been some part of me that had lots of built up anger inside. I was used to keeping my emotions in check by not expressing them to anybody or anything. I was good at keeping it to all myself. I thought that hiding my past and throwing the key into Pandora's box would be my solution. Then I'd be able to forget about everything and move on in my life without the worry of it coming back again. Of course, that wasn't the case.

Often, when something inside me triggered the memory of my drug addiction times, I would either feel ashamed or guilty. Other times, I would run away from it by doing something to keep me pre-occupied. I believe the challenges I was facing with the government was a test from the divine or the universe to see if I was ready to get to the next level in life.

As I was going through all these personal and human potential trainings, I realized that in life everything happens for reason. Whether it was good, bad, positive or negative, I was given choices in life. Look at it this way, I ended up owning a pharmacy that specialized in mental health and addiction services. The very people I was helping were the very reflection of who I used to be: a recovering drug addict who used to live in the Downtown Eastside. I held on to that part of my life so tightly because I felt guilty and ashamed of myself. I didn't want anyone to know. I was afraid they would think of me in a negative and fearful way.

While attending all those different workshops, something inside my gut started bubbling. My dark and traumatic past wanted to come out of my body, and I had a sudden urge to tell people about my past. I didn't know how or where it started. It was like the layers of an onion peeling away, one at a time. I started wondering what these feelings inside of me were and why they'd started to stir up after all these years.

In one of the training sessions, I was working on my chakra systems. There was one practice I did which involved me being fully immersed in the learnings and teachings of a mystery school. The first of four modules focused on my heart chakra; the chakra of love. I needed to harness this love so that I could forgive myself and others who bought hurt and emotional turmoil to me. In order for me to embrace and embody everything about me, whether it was good or bad, I needed to love myself fully and unconditionally. I had to bring in love and compassion in order to move on in my life.

After going through some of the trainings and having major breakthroughs and aha moments, I started informing my patients about my past life. I told them about being a drug addict and how I conquered my heroin addiction. I let it be known to some of my patients that their home in the Downtown Eastside used to be my home, too. Almost all of them were shocked to hear my story.

I continued telling my clients about my past, even though not all of them believed me. I had to show some of them the scars on my arms to confirm my tale. I wanted to reveal my haunting past to them because I wanted to inspire them to look to the positive, and to let them see that it *is* possible to get out of a life of addiction.

Reflection:

All the past events, all the traumas, all the highs and lows have shaped me into the person I am now. I believe I am on this planet to share my message with the world.

This world we are facing is filled with so much negativity, limiting beliefs, helplessness and hopelessness. But the world we are living in today doesn't have to be that way. We will always encounter challenges and hardships in our lifetime. But it's not these events that shape who we will become - it's the lessons we can learn from them.

A major lesson learned along the way of life is the choice to either get up after being knocked down or to simply stay down forever. I chose to get up and walk with even greater determination and I will continue to, so that I can live my life fulfilled.

The Final Fate of the Pharmacies

That year, we'd been faced with many changes, challenges and uncertainties in the pharmaceutical industry. The governing body of British Columbia basically ripped up the contract of the B.C. Pharmaceutical Services Act and introduced a newer version. Any pharmacy that wanted to continue doing business had to reapply to be enrolled in the new B.C. Pharmaceutical Services Act.

The agreement introduced new measures to give more power to the governing body, reducing our autonomy greatly. If we didn't enroll in the new Pharmaceutical Services Act, we wouldn't be able to continue our pharmacy practice. And if we didn't have an enrollment agreement with the BC government, the agreements we had in place with insurance carriers, such as Green Shield, Blue Cross and Assured Health, would be terminated.

Helen and I hired a lawyer to make sure we filled out the application properly. Some people were doing it on their own, which resulted in mistakes and delays in their enrollment process. Once our applications for the three stores were submitted, the waiting period began.

While we were at a training conference in California, I received news from the governing body about our enrollment. It was about ten 'o clock on a Friday night when I received the news, via email. Our request for the renewal of the agreement had been denied. My heart dropped to the floor. They gave us various reasons why they were denying us, and they also gave us three more desk audits, on top of the previous audits we were already dealing with.

The new audits stated we owed an *additional* $500,000 in errors. I was about to faint right then and there. Now we owed the government close to one million dollars. *How could this be*? It felt as though we were being targeted by the governing body. It felt like the story of David vs. Goliath.

So, we went for *another* round of battles with the government. We spent close to $100,000 in lawyer fees to seek an injunction so that the governing body would continue on with our enrollment without terminating the old one.

I asked many close friends to write character reference letters to present to the judge. I sought the help of friends who knew people in the government caucus, but it did not help. Finally, I asked the opposition party caucus for assistance, and they suggested I go to the BC ombudsman. If I went this route, then the opposition party could no longer help me, as it would be a conflict of interest.

From the time we received the letter of denial, we were given 21 days to write to the minister and plead our case. This was unsuccessful. They were determined to cancel our agreement with the government, which meant we would have to close down our business.

We had one last chance and I prayed it would work. We went to court to seek an injunction to grant us a hearing to proceed further, by challenging the administration. It took a couple of days for the judge to hear both sides of the arguments. Unfortunately, the judge was unable to provide an answer and we lost our case. We were done.

In order to repay what we owed to the government, we needed to sell all three of our stores. Because we lost the good-will part of the business, we could only sell our pharmacies for pennies on the dollar. I also had to sell the coffee shop for pennies on the dollar. It was just enough to pay everything back to the government. Closing down our stores was one of the hardest things I've ever had to do.

The entire process went on for almost three years. Three years of total chaos, uncertainty and negative emotions. And in the end, we lost close to a total of 1.5 million dollars. The whole thing created so much stress and disharmony in my life. It took a heavy toll on me, physically and mentally and put strain on my marriage.

The entire ordeal was a huge learning process for me. But I believe that having the ability to remain positive and open enabled me to see this experience differently than most people would. Some people I know who have been affected by changes in government regulations are now on medication to treat their depression. Others had to claim bankruptcy and were left with nothing. It's sad to see these people lose everything overnight. It's a scary prospect to think that an organization or someone in power has the ability to create so much chaos and turmoil in someone else's life. I am, therefore, extremely grateful that we survived the process.

Chapter 8: Where to Next?

The Present and Future

Despite all of the battles I'd experienced as a business owner, my life as an entrepreneur is still growing strong. My wife and I are now venturing into the wellness industry where I made a vow to the divine that I would inspire, empower and educate people to take charge of their health. I am now a much wiser and heart-centered person. The events in my life made me a better, stronger and more loving person. Even during the most challenging times, I did not give up on my family or myself, and I know I will continue to persevere and communicate my message to the world.

My new business is called Pure5 Wellness Hub. Our tag line is "Elevate your five senses by rejuvenating your mind, body and soul." In addition to taking self-improvement courses, I met a lady in my group from the Meaning Circle named Dr. Andrea Mills. She convinced me that since Helen and I opened our wellness center, I should embark on becoming educated in the field. Because I was determined to turn my life around, I acquired my Bachelor of Science in Holistic Health, in just under a year. My next goal is to pursue a PhD in Natural and Integrative Medicine.

Now, I would like to leave a message for you, the reader: When you find your way, your light will shine through and guide you to achieve abundance and your true happiness. Most importantly, do not ever lose sight of your dreams. If you need to find your way again, take a deep breath, close your eyes, put your hands on your heart and listen. Close your mind off to outside events and *really* listen to your heart, so you can find your passion and life's purpose.

I want to thank you for following my journey and ask that you please share my story so that others may also benefit and lead happier and more fulfilling lives.

Reflection: My last three nuggets for you

Nugget Number 8 I wish to share is that there are no distractions in life when you know your purpose and passion. Any distractions coming towards you will bounce right off. Because your determination is so strong, any wavering you do will only be temporary. If it becomes more nerve-racking, just pause what you're doing and take a few deep breaths. Once you've gotten your bearings, continue on your path.

Nugget Number 9 is to make your health a priority. I want to remind you of a famous quote, by A.J. Reb Materi: "So many people spend their health gaining wealth and then have to spend their wealth to regain their health." Therefore, it's imperative that we take care of ourselves in whatever form we can.

Stress is the number one leading cause of most diseases in our bodies. We need to be able to release the stress inside of us so our bodies can begin to heal whatever stressors there may be. One thing I learned through my teachings is to have "positive health." Dealing with circumstances, events and situations in a healthy and positive manner is paramount to one's well-being. Not only do we need to listen to our bodies, we need to tap into them by utilizing our five bodies of consciousness: our physical, vital, mental, supra-mental and bliss bodies.

The last nugget, Nugget Number 10, is to find a mentor. If you want to get the most out of life or to excel in whatever areas you are trying to achieve, then I strongly suggest you hire a mentor or coach to help you to reach your goals and aspirations. Make sure to check their references and their success rates.

A good coach or mentor will hold your ass to the fire and make sure you're getting things done and in a timely fashion. So, if you have the ability, hire one. You will not regret it. I have hired numerous coaches and mentors to make sure I am where I want to be, today.

Next Step

I currently reside in beautiful British Columbia, Canada, enjoying life and being of service to others. My passion is to help people take charge of their health, whether it's physically, emotionally or spiritually. I have learned to do so by hosting retreats, giving group talks and also by providing more private one-on-one interactions.

If you're looking to work with a coach or mentor, for help or manifestation of any sort, I would consider myself blessed to be the one you reach out to. I have made myself available through many platforms.

Please visit either of my websites at www.keithtongcoaching.com or www.keithtong.ca

You can also email me directly at keith@keithtongcoaching.com or keithtongcoaching@gmail.com

You may also contact me by visiting my Facebook or Instagram page at www.facebook.com/keith.tong.399 or www.instagram.com/t.keith.tong

Also, stay tuned, as I am in the process of re-branding the company with a new name: Total Vitality Centre. You will be able to visit our website soon, at www.totalvitalitycentre.com

Many Blessings.

Made in the USA
Monee, IL
02 August 2021